UNDERSTANDING THE CUSTOMER

For Karla

much love

Hilary

UNDERSTANDING THE CUSTOMER

THE ART OF SELLING

HILARY KENNY

LONDUBH BOOKS

First published in 2010 by

Londubh Books

18 Casimir Avenue, Harold's Cross, Dublin 6w, Ireland

www.londubh.ie

1 3 5 4 2

Cover by sinédesign

Origination by Londubh Books

Printed in Ireland by ColourBooks, Baldoyle Industrial Estate, Dublin 13

ISBN: 978-1-907535-06-2

For Jimmie, who sold me at first glance

ACKNOWLEDGEMENTS

Heartfelt thanks to Terry Prone, Chairperson of the Communications Clinic, sister, mentor and coach, whose encouragement and enthusiastic practical help added enormous value to this book. I ruthlessly exploited the expertise of Tom Savage, Anton Savage, Ger Kenny and Eoghan McDermott, and the long experience of the Communications Clinic staff, to come up with the suggestions and recommendations in it. The good stuff is theirs; the shortcomings are all mine.

Jerry Kennelly was especially generous in sharing his time, his wisdom and his down-to earth advice. Ann Heraty was, as always, gracious and helpful. And to the others, like Dervilla O'Brien and Noel Carr, whose wisdom I raided shamelessly, I'm very grateful.

Special thanks to Ger Kenny, always a calm, insightful and pragmatic adviser. I'm grateful for Eoghan McDermott's useful advice, drawn from his considerable experience. And to my editor, Jo O'Donoghue, I'm indebted for her thoroughly professional approach, coupled with immense patience in the face of delays.

CONTENTS

1

WHY AN IRISH BOOK ABOUT SELLING?

First of all, because Ireland is different. Different from any other country where you may get to try out your sales skills. Different in countless ways.

For starters, as this book goes to press, we're in an unprecedented downturn which makes selling anything more difficult – a lot more difficult – than it was a few years ago. At the beginning of the new millennium, the rising tide of the Irish economy had lifted every available boat. The nation was flush with cash and unashamed of spending it. Advertisements talked of 'must-have' items and customers went right along with that concept. Anybody could sell anything to anybody else, without much skill and without much attention to the price. All that has changed. Changed utterly. Surveys of consumer confidence reflect the unease people feel about the economy and about their personal finances. As individuals, they're markedly less likely to spend than they were just a few years ago.

It's much the same with business customers. Companies that, if they didn't quite do impulse buying three or four years ago, at least bought software, services and other items without asking too many questions, are now asking a rake of hard questions before they buy as much as a set of Tesco mugs to replace the chipped ones in the kitchen:

- How urgent is this purchase?
- Do we really need them/it?
- Could we postpone the purchase until the next quarter?
- Could people not buy their own?

The end result is like what happens when you run into the sea off a sloping beach: all speed and freedom until you hit the water and then everything slows almost to a halt.

The change, for salespeople in Ireland, is unprecedented. Up to recently, people who called themselves sales representatives were actually order-takers. They pitched up at the door of the target company, had a chat with the customer, took out their pad and happily made a list of the items the customer needed. It's not like that any more. That's why Chapter 2 deals with selling in a recession and how to reconstruct your approach if the old way no longer works for you.

The second reason Ireland needs a book on selling at this time is because Irish people communicate differently from people in other parts of the world. If you pick up a sales book in any Irish bookshop, you're likely to find that it comes from America or is heavily influenced by American salesmanship. Some of these books are very good – see the Bibliography on page 158 for a list of the better offerings. Some of them are very bad. But all of them are rooted in a cultural context that doesn't apply in this country. They recommend the asking of questions on which any

Irish salesperson would gag. Rightly gag. You can't take American questions and put them in Irish mouths – they'll be like failed dental implants: not effective for purpose.

Here's a common enough example. Several times in any one week, I prepare individuals to go for their first job, or for a promotion or career shift. It's not quite 'Lights, Camera, Action' but it's close to that. I interview them rigorously in front of a video camera, exploring their competencies, experience and expertise. Once, recently, I asked a young graduate where she would see herself in five years' time.

'Oh, in your job,' she responded brightly, referring to the deputy-chief-executive post held by the person I was representing in the interview.

When it came to playback, she positively glowed when we reached that point and produced a book out of her briefcase, with a title like *200 Great Interview Answers*. There it was, in the middle, described as 'a true killer answer.' Maybe in Boise, Idaho, it would be a killer answer. In Ireland, it would be an interview killer, because it's so obviously formulaic and so determinedly direct in its ambition, neither of which is warmly welcome in the Irish context.

Our manner of communication tends to be a bit more elliptical. The first time the consultants in my company fully realised just how elliptical Irish people are in their use of speech was when we trained foreign staff from an Irish multi-national. Halfway through the morning, when we checked how they were doing, one of the men said, with some relief, that at least he understood us. Since he had superb English, this threw us. Had he expected not to understand us? Silently, he turned his pad around so that we could see he had divided each page in two, one side devoted – as he explained – to noting 'Irish sayings that don't mean what they seem to mean.' We looked puzzled. The rest of the participants looked relieved. He had clearly hit a vein of shared experience.

The participants started to pepper us with words and phrases they had encountered and experienced difficulty with.

'Grand,' a Romanian woman offered.

Nods all around.

'I look up the dictionary, first time I hear 'grand' and find it a term of approval,' she said. 'It means big or – or...'

'Satisfaction,' another suggested.

'Satisfactory,' a third amended.

'Except that it means something completely different,' the Romanian went on. 'It is dependent on the tone. You give your report to the boss and she reads it and says, 'Grand,' and you know it is hateful to her. You ask her what is wrong with it and she says 'No, no, it's grand, I'll fix it later.' When the voice is down and sad and she says, 'Grand,' it means you have failed in so bad a way that she cannot even begin to explain it to you and would you go away please.'

At this point, a Spaniard who had been silent until then said that he had a different problem with 'grand.'

'What is, "Grand cake, Nora"?' he asked.

My younger colleagues looked at him blankly. So blankly that he became defensive.

'They say that in our department,' he told them. 'One woman says it all the time to everybody.'

I had to explain – to him and to the younger Irish people

present – that 'Grand cake, Nora' was a line from one of the first Irish TV soap operas, *The Riordans*. The farmer, Mr Riordan, would compliment his wife at tea time when she served him freshly-baked cake.

'Grand cake, Nora,' he'd say, before moving on to discussing the sarcoptic mange mites that were afflicting his flock. He said it so often that it became part of the Irish lexicon for a time. I explained to the Spaniard that whenever anybody used this phrase, things were going swimmingly.

'Swimmingly?' he asked, pencil in hand to make a note of my response.

Another participant commented that he found it difficult to work out what Irish people regarded as secret. In his early days in Ireland, he found colleagues to be startlingly open about their drinking habits, expenditure and attitudes. 'But,' he said, 'when I asked an Irish work colleague how she was going to vote, she looked at me as if I wanted to know who she went to bed with last night.'

A Dutch engineer asked what his boss meant when he told him, 'You're not doing yourself any favours.'

But the elliptical conversational style of the Irish went further than phraseology. One of the Polish participants said bitterly that, in his experience, Irish people would drag meetings on for hours, talking about irrelevancies rather than make a decision. This observation met with a chorus of agreement from the others.

Our great friend, Bunny Carr, once summed up this sideways approach to communication by remarking that the difference between an Irish audience and one from other countries was that the foreign audience listened to what you had to say, while the Irish audience tried to figure out what you were getting at.

This elliptical, indirect approach to communication means that the blunt selling methods advocated in many books and in some training programmes simply don't work in Ireland, whether in retail or in business selling.

Successful retail salespeople aim to develop relationships, however brief, with their customers, because they know that if they've served the customer well, repeat business often follows. How many of us who've been served in a slapdash, uninterested way will rush back to that shop? We certainly won't rush back to a shop where salespeople were actually rude to us. One chain in Ireland lost my business about twenty years ago for that reason. Last year they had a special range on sale and I broke my embargo and tried them again. Guess what: they'd learned nothing in the intervening decades. Their rude indifference to my enquiries resulted in my resumption of my boycott.

What's fascinating about this episode is that it indicates that some retail sales staff haven't got the message that there's a recession on. If they don't keep sales volumes up, they'll be laid off. If they don't sell more product than other salespeople, they'll be laid off. In good times, showing good manners and paying attention to the customer as a respected individual matters. In bad times, it's pivotal to survival in any retail sales business.

Paying attention is the key. Sales get lost in retail because, when a customer arrives in an area, the two employees present don't acknowledge her presence because they're too busy bitching to each other about the current roster. Sales get lost because a customer is left for ages while a salesperson fills in a form or sorts out her cash register. Instant, attentive helpfulness must be the watchword for anybody working in sales, whether retail or not.

Some branded goods have their own sales approach, which specifies particular behaviours at every stage of the sale. The Burberry franchises, for example, train all their associates to grab the client's interest, their attention, the moment they hove to. Sales people are taught to acknowledge the customer when they first come into the Burberry section of the sales floor, in a friendly professional way. Even if the sales assistant is with another client at the time, it's possible to make eye contact with a newcomer, and heavy stress is laid on doing just that in order to give the arriving customer a sense of being welcomed.

An experienced Burberry salesperson told me:

> To build up the client relationship is very important because most of the salespeople can make a sale to those customers who walk into the section; most people can do that as long as the customers have an interest in our products. What can make the salesperson stand out are the sales you can make to the clients who are not random customers. The salesperson who can build up a relationship with them and make them come back again, over and over, is the great salesperson. I wasn't able to do that at the very beginning, because where I used to work didn't have this kind of concept.
>
> But once I was trained everything changed.

I made sales of €7,000 to a group of Chinese tourists who came into Brown Thomas. In no more than a couple of hours. It was very interesting. About seven of them came in the group: it was very different from selling to Irish people because they're curious, and the way they buy and the way they behave are very different. Their requirements are different from those of Irish people. They want each purchase to be wrapped individually, each one with a separate receipt with the tax return form, and everyone's a little bit demanding and a bit impatient. I think I made the single highest sale that day.

The approach adopted by Burberry – and other durable brands – recognises that the easy part is selling to those people who just walk into the shop, but the objective has to be for each sales executive to develop a relationship with key clients. That means remembering, or being able to speedily access, each client's size, their preference in colours, their style. According to the Burberry salesperson, 'This will definitely increase the sales. Because the products are so expensive we are not always busy and when we are quiet we can take this time to build up the relationship with clients.'

In any area of retail or business selling, the crude hard sell is not likely to get you repeat business, let alone a long-term relationship. There's a fair build-up of evidence over the last few months to suggest that the hard sell is making a comeback in Ireland as desperation sets in and businesses lose focus on relationships and settle for one-off sales. A report in *The Irish Times* of 9 February 2010 about that lack of regulation of plastic surgery noted that patients were getting text messages saying they would be offered a discount if they hurried up and make their mind up to have the surgery.

It's astonishing that anybody providing a medical procedure as delicate and potentially dangerous as cosmetic surgery would engage in the dated techniques of the hard sell. Astonishing and lamentable. If someone is pressured into buying an overly expensive handbag or pair of shoes, they can bring them back and get a refund. If, on the other hand, a woman has a breast implant that leaves her scarred and sore or, worse still, infected, she's in a dire situation. Getting her money back is the least of her worries. She wants to get her body back and she may not be able to achieve it. The end results may be tragic.

The traditional old hard sell *can* work, in certain circumstances. It works when the target is insecure. It works when the target is easily bullied. It works when the target was going to buy anyway. In all those situations, the old ABC ploy – Always Be Closing – can do the trick. However, if you're trying to sell in Ireland, you have to remember that we are cynics and that we spot formulaic approaches a mile off. Formulaic approaches like what's been called the 'Ben Franklin Close,' whereby the salesperson writes down the pros and cons associated with the product or service on each side of a line down the centre of a page, always ensuring that the items on the positive side outnumber the negative. Or the assumption close, where the salesperson asks the customer, 'Would you like it in blue or red?'

The hard sell doesn't work for any important sale. It doesn't take account of the human emotions involved. Buyers must want and need the product or service you supply. And if they report to someone else, like a board or a CEO, they have to convince them what a good deal it is. And make them feel good, too.

Unless the context makes the hard sell work. Last year, I wandered into the Better Homes and Gardens exhibition in the RDS. Meandering between stands, I found myself at an improvised stage in the middle of one aisle. On it, an Englishman was flogging a metal and plastic gadget for shredding carrots – not something any of the people present had an immediate and pressing need for. But we stopped and listened, because it was such a performance. He first of all told us how, whenever we had a dinner party, we looked up recipes, loved the pictures of dishes beautifully garnished and either abandoned the idea because we knew we'd never shred enough carrots thinly enough for them to look good, or tried it with a sharp knife and ended up bleeding into the vegetables and welcoming guests covered in Elastoplast. Those around the stage laughed and nodded. Then he demonstrated his solution. Fast. Simple. Fluid.

Each of us thought, 'Yeah but you do this every day, it wouldn't be that easy for the rest of us.'

He stopped in mid-action and surveyed us all. 'Know what you're finking,' he announced. 'You fink it's easy for me 'cos I do it all the time, right?'

Another laugh. He dragged an elderly woman up the steps on to the stage and – his hand over hers – showed her how to use it. 'Now, you do it,' he ordered.

Within seconds, she was producing long, feathery

fragments of carrot. He had some difficulty getting her back off the stage, she was so happy with the end result. Then he showed us all the other things the gizmo could do. Finally, he hammered home that for a ridiculously small price, you would get a carrot-fragmenter, plus...plus...plus so much more for free. You wouldn't get one extra attachment. You wouldn't get two extra attachments. You would get three extra attachments. Not to mention a wonderful recipe book that would transform your reputation as a culinary performer.

He then shunted the group into a line in front of the cash register, where a young woman took the money and handed over the plastic and metal gadgets in cute bags, while he continued to confirm for the purchasers that they were the cleverest people this side of Beijing.

It was a tour de force, made more acceptable by the allowances everybody made for his bullying, over-the-top outrageousness – he was English, after all. People were out for the day, he was entertaining and repetitive and, because the item was cheap to start with, nobody had to worry that the purchase would beggar them. They all knew damn well, as they walked away with their bags, that the gadget would gather dust at the back of a cupboard – but so what?

The point is that this man's selling technique was acceptable in context but would be neither acceptable nor effective if, for example, he was selling a software programme allied to training designed to make a company compliant with health and safety regulations. It wouldn't be acceptable, because the latter product/service is what's called a 'strategic sale.'

A strategic sale requires significant expenditure on

the part of the purchaser and/or significant change in the way the employees within the purchasing company work. Nobody achieves a strategic sale by getting a little old lady to try out the technology or yelling about the three extra attachments that come for free. Strategic selling is a science involving top-level interrogation, listening and relationship-building. It will be covered in great detail in this book, because it's the most important kind of selling as a career: it's infinitely varied, allows for the generation of substantial profits and creates the context for many further sales to the same purchaser.

We looked at some of the challenges Ireland presents as a country in which to sell; let's look at the advantages. One significant aspect of business in Ireland is the scaling down of the 'six degrees of separation' concept, the idea that only six people separate an individual from any other individual on the planet. In John Guare's play of this name, first performed in 1990, a character muses:

> I read somewhere that everybody on this planet is separated by only six other people. Six degrees of separation. Between us and everybody else on this planet. The president of the United States. A gondolier in Venice. Fill in the names. I find that a) tremendously comforting that we're so close and b) like Chinese water torture that we're so close. Because you have to find the right six people to make the connection.

In Ireland you may find that far fewer than six degrees separate you from the person you want to meet. Try it for yourself. How many moves would it take to get you to the Kerry footballer, Paul Galvin? I bet you wouldn't need six.

This is a blessing and a curse. We all know someone who knows someone who knows a guy – and so on. It's a blessing from the selling perspective, because you can nearly always find someone in a position to help you with an introduction to a buyer in a company. The curse sets in if (a) you mess up or (b) if one of the links in the chain doesn't like you. The first is more important. Getting around the missing link is relatively easy – you can find another approach to your desired target. Messing up, on the other hand, carries far-reaching consequences. Remember, if someone has done you the favour of introducing you to a potential client, they don't want that potential client to go back to them asking why they inflicted a disorganised unprofessional moron on them.

This book aims to help you not to mess up. If you do, it aims to show you how to fix the problem in such a fast and effective way that the customer will be a friend for life. Interestingly, studies show that customers who've had a problem fixed are far more loyal (some research says 85 per cent more) than customers who've had standard good service without any problems.

Another major reason for an Irish book on selling is the disproportionate number of small and medium enterprises in Ireland. The number of big organisations (typically the ones that have dedicated sales departments) is a tiny minority (just 3 per cent of the overall figure.) Over 97 per cent of businesses operating in Ireland today are 'small': they employ fewer than fifty people. There are approximately a quarter of a million small businesses in

Ireland, employing 777,000 people. Many of these firms employ just one or two people in sales.

We in the Communications Clinic have noticed that those one or two individuals in sales tend to become isolated from the rest of the staff. Even in large firms, salespeople get cut off from the rest of the company. They may not get the kind of back-up they need to cement relationships.

This could be fatal. All companies, but especially small to medium outfits, need to infect every member of staff with the selling bug. Every time a staff member picks up the phone to anyone, their greeting must be cheerful, their approach helpful and their follow-up fast and efficient – that's what predisposes towards sales. People sell to people. We all need to do it, every day.

Now, stop and read that last paragraph again, because it hits another key reason for an Irish book about selling. Or, rather, two reasons. Irish people rarely describe themselves as 'engaging in sales' and if they're not directly involved in flogging something, they assume they have no function whatever in the sale.

Neither is true. All of us sell all the time. We sell ideas to each other. The payoff may be the satisfaction of having informed or persuaded someone else. Or it may be in changed behaviour: your mate gets sold on the idea of putting out the wheelie bin or putting the dishes in the dishwasher.

It's the same in companies. In really great, customer-focused companies, everybody, whether client-facing or in a back room in an administrative role, understands that they have a selling role:

- In their supportive interaction with the salespeople
- When they encounter a potential customer outside office hours
- In maintaining the company's brand and image at all times

In those companies, the job of the salesperson is made easier by the conviction of each employee that he or she contributes to the final sale and the satisfaction they take in contributing to it.

This book is not about marketing or merchandising. These are separate and different – and extraordinarily important – disciplines. Most successful selling occurs only as a consequence of effective marketing and we take that as a given. The book is about helping you to see that sales are *your* responsibility, regardless of advertising, merchandising or marketing. Indeed, it's everyone's job to sell, whether you're the CEO or the tea-lady. I remember vividly catering staff who looked after me kindly and smilingly – they made a huge impression on behalf of their company.

In the end people sell to people – even in the days of the Internet, Amazon and eBay. People go back to e-sources for goods only if they've been satisfied with the service they received – did the book arrive in time; was it the right one; was the payment processed efficiently; if there were problems, were they dealt with adequately and promptly?

Strategic selling is inextricably interwoven with service. Follow up a sale with bad service and, even if your customers swallow their complaint and fail to articulate it to you or to anybody else, you won't get another order from them.

Within this book, you'll find practical, proven methods of improving your selling skills, or getting you started if you have no such skills. What you won't find are tricks designed to turn you into a stereotypical salesperson. Because that never works in Ireland. An Irish person will hear you coming from two miles off and instantly reject the distinctive formulaic phrases of a learned-off approach to closing the sale.

This book is about achieving success at authentic, ethical selling. And about having fun while you're at it. It gives you a step-by-step approach to follow, taking you from your very first thoughts to finally closing the sale. Your first thoughts are when you sit back and consider: of all the businesses and potential customers out there, who is most likely to be helped by the product or service I have to offer?

At this point, you haven't even started prospecting: you're still trying to narrow down the great world out there into possible customers. You'll come up with a big list of possibles, research them and filter them into a smaller list of prospects, then plan your cold calls. Cold calls will be followed by information-gathering meetings (with an even smaller number of potential customers), putting proposals together, making your pitch and closing the deal.

All that early filtering and research, up to the planning of the cold call, we can call stage 1. Stage 2 is the cold call and the follow-up to the cold call, including the data-collecting and information-gathering meeting/s. Stage 3 kicks in when you and the customer are much clearer about how you can help them: this is where you put the formal proposal together. After they receive the proposal they ask you to pitch (if you've done your work well): this is Stage 4. And Stage 5 is when you make the final adjustments and close the sale. The five different stages of the strategic sales process are sometimes represented by a funnel diagram, as below.

Follow the stages we recommend, fully and with energy and enthusiasm, and you will certainly be a better salesperson. Enjoy.

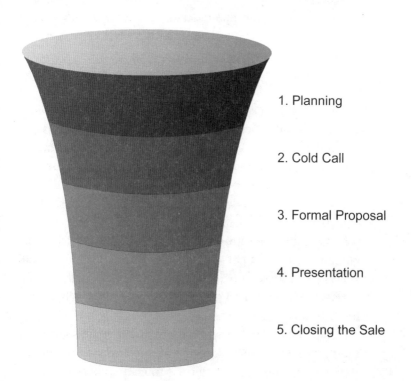

1. Planning

2. Cold Call

3. Formal Proposal

4. Presentation

5. Closing the Sale

SELLING IN A RECESSION

A recession creates its own myths, not least of them the belief that one identifiable person or group of people is to blame for the downturn. Some of the myths that develop about the problems of doing business in a recession are true. Some are not true. And some are irrelevant.

RECEIVED WISDOM 1: IN A RECESSION, SALES STAGNATE
True. Not all sales but many sales. Some companies do better in a downturn. In March, 2010, for example, McDonald's announced that they were opening four new outlets in Ireland, delivering about two hundred jobs, because they were doing nicely, thank you. The CEO of the company credited the cost-effectiveness of their offering for the results, pointing out that a basic burger from the golden arches company cost €1 three years ago and still costs just €1 today. No doubt he has a point – furthermore, it was observed, long ago, that in a recession, people buy more burgers, more beer and more pills.

Once the current downturn began, the most significant stagnation was immediately evident in big-ticket items, starting with houses. Once the property bubble burst, we quickly learned a new phrase: negative equity. Negative equity occurs when houses stop selling. The end result is that the house you bought for €300,000 and planned to sell for €400,000 to move up the property ladder is now worth two-thirds of what it used to be worth. If you're lucky. It could now be worth half what it cost you. But you still have to pay the mortgage as if the value hadn't changed. Banks are like that. Inflexible.

Directly after negative equity set in, sales of cars plummeted. As painful fiscal measures kicked in, drivers who had planned to buy a new car at the top of the year decided they could wait for another twelve months. Or, in some cases, decided that they had no choice but to wait for that period. And when the twelve months were up, many of them went a step further, hung on to the car and resigned themselves to straightening its crooked headlights in advance of the NCT. The jury is still out on the capacity of scrappage schemes to stimulate car sales significantly

The drop in car sales was exacerbated by a bizarre form of downward mobility, which led people who could afford to buy, say, a 2010 car, not to invest in one, lest they be perceived by their poverty-stricken neighbours as getting above themselves. The consequences for the car industry were horrific. Many of the best-known retailers went under, while others went through radical retrenchment.

Anybody who did buy a big-ticket item shopped around and did endless price-comparisons before they put their money down. People were suddenly doing what the former Tánaiste, Mary Harney, had once been ridiculed for advising them to do – shopping around.

During the boom years, shopping around took up more

time than it seemed to be worth, because we were cash-rich and time-poor. When the economy went belly-up, many people became cash-poor and time-rich. Thousands emigrated. Thousands more joined the dole queues. Newspapers were largely kept afloat by the full page advertisements taken out by TESCO, Supervalu, Dunnes Stores and others, pointing out how incredibly cheap they were for the basic goods every household needs every week. Lidl and Aldi became shops of choice. People abandoned expensive brands and learned to love obscure versions of the same product.

Teetotalers like me were convinced, as we passed pubs on Thursday and Friday evenings, that drinkers were still finding the cash to buy drink but in fact the figures show that drink sales dropped by as much as 10 per cent in the year to March 2010.

At first, it seemed as if coffee shops would be exempt from this trend, because the addiction built up over the boom years did not seem likely to wane. Coffee shop owners, however, noticed behaviour changes early on. One of my customers, who owned a coffee shop that was part of an international franchise operation, told me about the day he spotted the difference:

> The day I knew that times were getting rough was the morning I walked in and noticed a significant difference in the way the people in the queue were standing. I was delighted, at first, to see a good long queue, coming, as I was, from my car where *Morning Ireland* was depressing me about the economy. Then I realised that

every person had in their hand a pile of change
that added up to the cost of a beaker of coffee.
Up to that point, they'd have had a hand in their
pocket, ready to yank out notes, not just for their
latte but to cover the cost of a muffin, a tin of
mints or a panini.

It was the beginning of an enormous change, a change
that many coffee shops responded to pretty quickly, not by
dropping their prices but by offering 'sandwich and coffee'
deals you couldn't have got a year earlier. At the beginning
of 2010, even this wasn't enough and some well-known and
well-loved coffee shops became extinct. Every day brought
its story of a once-crowded restaurant closing down. Hotel-
owners made no secret of the great difficulties in which
they found themselves.

Skinny lattes and weekends away are luxury items. They
may not have seemed like luxuries in the days before the
stripes fell off the Celtic Tiger but the fact is that neither
is essential to life. However cars *are* essential, in the many
areas of the country poorly served by public transport, but
people are making do with last year's model, because it's a
big outlay and no one knows for sure when the downturn
is going to bottom out. If you're still in a job but you're not
sure for how long, you're going to husband your resources
and save on big expenditure, in case in three months' time
you have to live for the rest of the year on what the new car
would have cost. No amount of sales expertise can dent
that decision.

So a salesperson in the new-car business faces a task
roughly akin to climbing a frozen waterfall while covered

in bacon fat, and anybody selling anything other than Big Macs faces a similar if slightly less daunting challenge. Them's the breaks and now is the time to look at your optimism levels. Because this situation is not going to go away in the short term.

RECEIVED WISDOM NUMBER 2: IN A DOWNTURN SALES BECOME PARTICULARLY PRICE-SENSITIVE

Yes, but only in the short term. At a certain point, prices can't sink any lower, because selling at a loss solves only liquidity problems. If it costs you €30 to make a skirt and you've been selling skirts for €100, you can afford to shift a lot of stock for €50 each. You can even afford to reduce them below cost, to say €20 each, if you must secure cash to meet immediate expenses.

What this does, though, is simply meet the urgent crisis. It leaves you with no reserve to pay for any new stock you've ordered. It also affects customer perceptions. They think, 'Last month I paid €100 for that and now they're only charging $20. Some mark-up. Think I'll move to Penneys.'

Some prices don't respond to recessionary pressures. For example, ticket prices for the 2009 Slane concert were not reduced at all. And the young staff in the office tell me that while Oxegen said they kept the 2009 prices at the 2008 level, this wasn't much use to people who could have had the same acts while camping in Spain for not much more than a third of the price. In fact the Spain deal covered four days of acts, as opposed to three in Ireland, and nine days camping as opposed to just three in Ireland.

In the services area, pressure on price has grown over the last eighteen months. Some of that pressure has come from companies reducing, say, their advertising spend. It doesn't matter how well a salesperson from the advertisement agency dances in front of them: if the managers of a company are facing insolvency, they're going to cut whatever they can as long as it doesn't precipitate the closing of their business. Advertising is the easiest and most illogical cut. Next easiest and equally illogical is PR (because PR budgets are much lower than advertising budgets). Third and most illogical is training.

The reality is that, whatever else is cut, communication should not be. And whatever else you cut, you should not cut training. Training is not a luxury. Training is what will make your staff better at what they do. If they're better at what they do, your bottom line will improve. It's a no-brainer and a total misunderstanding of which spend is discretionary and which is essential. That's my rant over. But the problem remains: when companies are in trouble, they cut the obvious and immediate in a radical way, instead of more subtly attacking the hidden costs that accrete throughout the good years. Externally provided services are among the most obvious and immediate targets for cutbacks, which in turn spells horror for advertisement agencies, conference organisers, PR consultancies, event managers and training firms. Even the most radical price-slashing won't persuade companies caught in a cashflow log-jam to relax their ban on services.

Some service companies in the 'soft and fuzzy' areas have resorted to savage cost-cutting but in areas like event-management, cost-cutting has its limitations, as third-party charges like venue hire and catering represent so much of the bill going to the client.

The bottom line is that too many service-suppliers, whether they're individuals or larger companies, have been panicked by the downturn into one of two actions: radical cost cuts or more anxious knocking on doors. Anyone trying to sell services in a downturn needs to change their point of view. Instead of starting from where they're at, they need to start with where the potential client is at and work out what, if anything, the service supplier can do to solve the potential client's problems. Repeated cold-calling backed by discounts aren't selling. They're the pointless manifestations of desperation.

RECEIVED WISDOM NUMBER 3: IN A RECESSION, COMPETITION INCREASES

Yes, and how companies and organisations handle this pressure fundamentally affects their pricing.

Even if it means making short-term losses, many companies will set out to wallop the opposition by under-cutting them and building their own market share. Take cars, for example. You'd never have considered a Citroën before this year – now you have one. What the car industry knows is that brand loyalty in the sector is strong: once you find a make that suits you, you stick to it (ask your husband). Manufacturers are hoping that once you make the brand switch they will keep your loyalty, patricularly if you are a first-time car-buyer going for a dirt-cheap option from them.

On the other hand, some companies, particularly in the service area, take a far-sighted view of recession. They don't apply a slash and burn approach to cutting costs. They realise that this can lead to anomalies: prices are reduced but without clarity about the direction in which the short-term and long-term goals of the organisation lie. Another danger of opportunistic price-reductions is that Client A finds out that Client B is being charged much less for the same service.

Adopting a purely cashflow approach can lead very quickly to a hand-to-mouth situation that does nothing for quality and product development. Staff have to be let go suddenly, because there's no medium-term plan, never mind a long-term one. Firms that take a strategic view will work out how they can retain their best staff in a variety of circumstances. They'll have a stepped approach to dealing with dropping revenue. We've seen some firms first seek a salary cut. Their next step might be to let some of the newer staff go. Then they'll offer unpaid summer leave or sabbaticals to more of their staff. Shorter working hours might follow. They'll do everything they possibly can to retain staff rather than let key personnel go. These staff members are so valuable to them that they will want to use them to rebuild the company when the upturn comes. The last thing they want to do is lose them to a rival.

The aim of business is to make a profit. If staff retention becomes the aim, trying to make a profit as well is hard. The slash and burn approach doesn't take account of who is key to the firm's survival and development. Nor does it factor in how staff retention will affect profit and for how long. It may involve senior people taking on tasks that aren't cost-effective, while missing the chance to do serious marketing and selling. And really important staff members, who earn more than newer recruits, may have to be let go because the comany didn't plan for a range of contingencies. Or they may leave, to go to an organisation that seems to appreciate their value. In all these situations, sales assume a new importance.

RECEIVED WISDOM NUMBER 4: IN A RECESSION, RELATIONSHIPS MATTER MORE

In spades. Here's where the salesperson who has nurtured relationships comes into his or her own. It doesn't mean they'll get more sales. What it does mean is that they're the ones who will get whatever sales are going, however few they may be. The salesperson who genuinely cares about customers and stays in contact with them tends to end up with customers enough to keep his company ticking over.

Picture this. Your company has been warned to cut costs in every department and activity. No new purchases at any price without checking with the Chief Financial Officer. And then the server goes down. Are you going to start phoning round for the lowest offer? If your company is sensible, it will have done this a long time before, weighing the price against the service and awarding the work to the firm with the best balance.

We have a support company that went to great lengths to identify and fix an IT problem for us some months ago. They met with all kinds of obstruction from our IT provider but maintained the relationship with them until they could sort out our problem. We're now doubly sure of their commitment. We wouldn't dream of switching even in the teeth of stern CFO warnings because we can rely on them. That's worth a lot of cash. Just as importantly, it means a lot of time saved for us to serve our clients, time that would otherwise have been spent in shopping around.

One of the bad things that happened during the boom years was the corruption of the word 'relationship.' Instead, for example, of 'after-sales service,' people talked about 'relationship management.' It's a bit like the nonsense that was talked about corporate values during the same period. Corporate values were claimed by companies, on websites and in annual reports, as if they could be confected over a weekend spent discussing the corporate mission statement. The reality is that values, by their nature, emerge from the constantly repeated actions of a company, not from an aspirational statement dreamed up by the management. Values are defined by the way we live, not the claims we make about ourselves.

In the same way, 'relationship-building' was talked of as if it were a mechanical process. Executives were sent on training courses purporting to establish steps to a good relationship. One of the steps was a process called 'mirroring.'

Mirroring is based on the observation that when people like each other, they unconsciously tend to mimic one another's physical behaviours. For example, if you notice, in the course of a night out, that you and your date are taking sips from your wine glass or cider flagon at the same time, you are probably doing well.

The trick, executives (particularly sales executives) were told, was constantly to adopt the posture of the other person. A relationship would follow, as day follows night.

The fallacy of this approach derives from confusing cause and effect. People may pick up the gestures and posture of others as a consequence of feeling close to them but this doesn't mean that mimicking the gestures and posture of another individual will result in their feeling close to you.

If you try to make sure you mirror your date, you'll end up concentrating on that rather than engaging with the person sitting opposite you. Real relationships, in the selling business or in any business, are fostered by respect, attention, suppression of the natural instinct to show off and remembering what's important about the other person. Not by learning mechanical tricks.

RECEIVED WISDOM NUMBER 5: AFTER-SALES SERVICE BECOMES MORE IMPORTANT

When a company is growing rapidly, it tends to develop a 'Toss it and forget it' attitude to products or services that don't deliver. Microsoft's Vista was a classic example. It was installed in computer systems all over the world or came pre-installed on new computers. Users didn't like it. It failed to deliver what they expected. When a new, improved, more intuitive version of Windows came along, they ditched VISTA and migrated to it, without going through much of a grieving process about the system that had, essentially, failed to meet their needs.

Similarly, when an advertisement campaign failed to deliver what had been expected of it, another was created to replace it. Or if a training programme didn't kick up the hoped-for results, the person in HR shrugged and bought another.

Microsoft didn't suffer permanent reputation damage as a result of the Vista years, not least because those years coincided with a period of benign pressure, when everybody was doing well. This pattern held in many areas of business. The economic downturn brought a new focus on cost-containment and a matching abandonment of the 'Toss it and forget it' mentality. Since 2008, businesses have placed a higher value on ensuring that products and services actually work the way they're supposed to work. They also want products to work for longer and to have the capacity to be updated, rather than replaced.

This is bad news for commodity-sellers whose profit comes from flogging an item to a large number of customers they'll encounter once and once only. It's good news for salespeople who provide a product or service to customers with whom they hope to be engaged over the long term. Because, as the emphasis on after-sales service becomes more pronounced, so does the opportunity to continue to provide products or services to that customer.

Selling a product shouldn't end abruptly once money changes hands – not if you want to make subsequent sales. You should always follow up, to check if any difficulties have arisen or if anything extra would add value.

If your customer has had a problem with your product or service, you must fix it, right now. You'll find out exactly what's wrong so your fix is appropriate and complete. You will apologise and take the blame, even if the fault was with an incomplete or incorrect brief from them. You'll ask their advice about the solution you propose – people love to be asked for advice. You will check that the solution worked out. You will leave no trace of dissatisfaction, so that when the next sale opportunity arises, you'll be thought of immediately and with goodwill.

The more stroppy among you will be asking yourselves 'Why should I take the blame if it wasn't my fault?' You may even be concerned that doing this will damage you and your company in the perception of the customer. You may suspect that the customer is thinking about you, 'What an idiot – he didn't get it wrong – my boss changed the brief later and I have to stay on the right side of my boss, so I couldn't admit that.'

Our decades-long experience is that if you take the blame, at worst the customer will gloss over the whole blame/responsibility area, moving rapidly to solutions. Sometimes, the customer will confess that he hadn't remembered all the parameters but that he can't officially say that, showing his appreciation of your willingness to shoulder responsibility. You can then reciprocate with an acknowledgement of your mutual desire to get it right this time and asking for any other suggestions to this end.

At best, as happened to me last year, the customer immediately responded to my guilty plea with, 'No, not your fault at all. Our mistake entirely. Thank you for being so ready to put it right.' Now you're in partnership with the organisation you're selling to – and being in partnership is the very definition of relationship selling.

You can see that selling in a recession is even more dependent on relationships. A really important task to add to your 'To Do' list in a downturn is keeping in touch with contacts, with the added value of searching out, even more actively, the opportunities to be helpful.

Too often, salespeople construe 'being helpful' as restricted to their own product or service. It isn't. If you can put Joe in touch with Jennifer who may have an opening in her company or a need for Joe's new product, this has no immediate crude benefit to you or your company but it is genuinely helpful to your client. It's doing what you would do for a friend, except for someone who is not – yet – a friend. It's doing the right thing without manipulative intent.

If it has any immediate payoff, that payoff lies in feeling better about yourself because you know what you've done is useful to the other person. Because it serves the other person's needs without arriving with the hook of your needs or wants attached, the other person is likely to trust you more.

That's how friendships happen. Being friends with a customer is important, in purely human terms. Customers are not 'prospects.' They're people, with all the complexities, potential, hopes, dreams and problems you have. Treating them as people, rather than as a means to personal advancement or profit, responding to them as you would to a friend rather than as a target, will change your business life for the better. It will reduce the chances of your waking each morning with a heavy dread inside you at the prospect of a day ahead filled with unpleasant encounters with powerful figures who may reject you. It will improve your self-esteem, not because you're notching up sales but because you simply like yourself more.

At some point, as a result of your intervention, Jennifer or Joe may think of you and your company when they need your service or product. You have no way of measuring this likelihood and even *trying* to measure it doesn't make sense. In non-business relationships, we expend emotional energy and time on people who matter to us without ever sitting down to measure the outcome. A friend of mine who works in an advertising agency planned a birthday present for her boyfriend and booked flights for a romantic weekend in Paris for the two of them. All aglow with her cunning plan, as yet unrevealed to him, she got a bright idea as to how she might tell him. She talked to a graphic artist and between them they mocked up a proposal just like the proposals they'd normally make to a prospective client, illustrating the benefits of the weekend in Paris in business language. The end result was ironic and funny and added greatly to the birthday package. She got a kick out of doing it. He got a kick out of receiving it.

Taking this kind of care of a client helps to turn them into a friend. And both business life and selling are lot more pleasant when you're dealing with friends.

RECEIVED WISDOM NUMBER 6: EVERYBODY'S UNDER PRESSURE

That's a fact. But it can also be an advantage. Pressure can push you into running faster on the same hamster wheel or it can prompt you to rethinking your priorities.

Recession-created pressure is handled best by people who can get off the wheel of routine and establish which bits of their daily activities are unproductive. In this sense, recession can be a good thing.

It can also be a good thing when salespeople and service providers are able to respond to customers who themselves are under pressure and provide a product or service that can help them out of a jam.

A former boss of mine, Bunny Carr, started his business in the teeth of the recession of the 1970s and made an enormous success out of the venture. When that recession was at its deepest, one of the company's directors looked at the books and was agreeably surprised by what she found there.

'I don't understand how we're doing so well,' she remarked, 'when so many companies are going under or just hanging on by their fingernails.'

'Always remember one great truth about communications consultancy,' Bunny replied. 'It's when people are in dire straits that they reach out to us for help getting finance, staving off debtors, winning new business or talking to their staff about downsizing. If they weren't under pressure, they wouldn't need us.'

People who do not have the natural instincts of a born salesperson figure that if customers are under pressure, they haven't the time to meet a salesperson or the money to spend on what the salesperson is offering, so what's the point?

The point is that if you're selling Ferraris or Louis Vuitton luggage, it's not realistic, in the middle of a recession, to expect a plethora of customers ready to make an impulse buy once they put their bottom on the soft leather car seat for a test drive, or once you get them to heft the classy Louis Vuitton overnight valise.

On the other hand, two interlinked human needs come to the fore in a recession; the need to save money and the need to save time. If you and your product or service can be shown to do both, a recession may be a great time for you. At the very least, you're likely to get your 'Yes' or 'No' more quickly than a few years ago.

RECEIVED WISDOM NUMBER 7: IT'S A WHOLE NEW WORLD OUT THERE

Not really. The economy still has its nose in the gravel. Emigration is on the increase. The dole queues are appallingly long. People have less money and what money they have, they're holding on to.

But the needs of industry are constant. Unchanging. Businesses need to make a return on investment. Profit, in other words. In order to make profit, they have to create turnover. In order to create turnover, they have to find people who want what they have to offer and sell it to them. The need for focused, ethical, relationship-based salesmanship goes up, rather than down, in a recession.

If you're energetic, optimistic and a good listener who genuinely likes people, you can be as successful in sales in a recession as you would be in more buoyant financial times.

But, because it's not all about you, we should, first of all, look at your customer. Or potential customer.

Because that's where all selling starts. Not with you. Or your product or service. But with the customer.

3

THE RESEARCH STAGE:
IT'S NOT ALL ABOUT YOU, YOUR
COMPANY OR YOUR SERVICE

It's dead easy to get a list of target companies, broken down by turnover, level of employment or function. Those lists can be helpful to a salesperson, if only to prevent a seller trying to flog a milking machine to a newspaper proprietor or a computer server to a new mother.

It's dead easy to click on the website of any one of those companies. It can be helpful, too, if only to give you a sense of how the company likes to view itself.

It's dead easy to email the company or telephone them to find out the name of the purchasing or procurement or training or development manager or director.

And with these three chunks of data under their belt, this, as far as most salespeople are concerned, is the time to call out 'Lights! Camera! Action!'

They're right, if what they're selling can be purchased, right off the bat, by the person who's agreed an appointment with them. If it's not going to cost more than a couple of hundred Euro, doesn't demand down time on the part of the company or a division within it and doesn't require extensive retraining of staff followed by a completely different way of doing things. If these circumstances apply, what has happened is an easy-peasy impulse buy. The buyer will not have sleepless nights worrying if the thing will overheat, underperform or require constant expensive updates. They can forget the seller and the seller can forget them.

Not many companies employ sales staff in the easy-peasy impulse buy department any longer because eBay, Amazon, Spiegel and a million other websites now cater so perfectly for the impulse buyer that they don't even have to go to the front door of their own house in order to talk to the salesperson. They can click on a item and follow instructions so that the goods arrive within days, bubble and shrink-wrapped into inert safety within save-it-for-later cardboard packaging.

Easy peasy sales led to order-takers kidding themselves that they were ace salespeople. If, for example, you represent a book wholesaler like Easons, you're not going to have to kill yourself to get a bookshop to stock the latest Cathy Kelly novel or Malcolm Gladwell non-fiction offering. Both are going to float off the shelves into the willing hands of readers. It's a matter of taking the order and working out how many the bookseller will shift before your next visit. The bookshop owner knows that if you turn out to be wrong, all he has to do is ship the three copies of the book he ordered right back to the publisher. He won't be out of pocket. That's one of the peculiarities of bookselling. Initial orders from bookshops may be encouraging but if the books don't sell to readers, they are returned and the picture represented by the initial healthy orders can begin to look very different very quickly.

(And if you're planning to write a bestseller, look out for a new edition of the classic *Write and Get Paid for It* by my colleague, Terry Prone, recently published by Londubh Books. It will fill you in on how to sell your own book. To a publisher. And through media appearances.)

Like most other businesses, the book trade has taken a hell of a knock in recent times, not just because of the recession but because people can read so many books, free, on their computer, through sites like the Gutenberg Project, buy them through Amazon or download them at a discount to their Kindle or Sony e-reader. February 2010 saw the Hughes and Hughes chain go into receivership and, nationwide, order-takers are leaving bookshops with smaller orders.

This pattern has seeped into other businesses, including medicines. Most of the major pharmaceutical manufacturers in Ireland employ their own sales teams and these sales teams have found the ground shifting beneath their feet in recent times, although not, in the main, as a result of recession. In the case of medicines, the 'gateway buyer' is a general practitioner or a hospital consultant. An ordinary person may buy over-the-counter (OTC) medicines like Panadol without prescription but they are not permitted to purchase Prozac or Augmentin without the intervention of a GP or specialist and so it's to the doctor's office that the salesperson from the pharmaceutical company calls when they have product to sell.

My company does an enormous amount of business training sales representatives from these companies and every one of them has reported the same trend to us: whereas in the past pharmaceutical reps were little more than sample-droppers and order-takers, their task is now much more challenging. They find it difficult to get appointments with doctors and when they do get appointments, the medics are often impatient and inattentive. When we train those reps, we present them, not with role-play, which we find to be limited in its utility, but with real GPs or hospital consultants. They quickly learn how much medical professionals hate being subjected to 'the spiel.' That often comes as a shock to them, because old-style medical rep training concentrated almost completely on the development and refinement of that spiel. The rep was rated, in training, on how, no matter how pressured the encounter, they managed to 'put across they key messages' the company wanted inserted in the medic's head.

Medical professionals subjected to spiel-givers quickly learned a) to hate the spiel-giver and, by extrapolation, to hate their company and their product and b) that the quickest way to end the encounter was to sit in silence, ideally while undertaking some other task, and let them get on with it.

'They want to treat me like an inanimate stump, I'll make like an inanimate stump,' was how one specialist summed up the process.

Of course, medical reps do not wants their potential gateway purchasers to behave like inanimate stumps. They want to be trusted by the medical professionals. They don't want to waste the professionals' time, so that the next occasion they pitch up in his or her office, they will be welcomed, rather than suffered, engaged with, rather than tolerated, allowed to add value rather than just get through guff. But they want to achieve much more than this already ambitious goal. They want to be seen as the personification of a company with standards and solutions that listens to medical practitioners, pays attention to what they learn by listening and responds to issues raised.

This means treating each individual practitioner as an individual: observing them, copping on to their needs, their likes, their dislikes, their habits of mind, their attitudes and the regional or practice peculiarities they face. This requirement means a sea change from order-taking to action research, as each medical rep has to, effectively, learn to profile each and every GP and specialist and respond respectfully and intelligently to their specific needs. I'm talking about the advance research any salesperson can do in advance of their first encounter with a potential customer, whether that potential customers is a GP or the HR manager of a multi-national.

In the case of the latter, a good salesperson doesn't set out on the initial cold call without finding out, inter alia, the following:

- How's the company doing?
- How is it managed?
- What's special, new or different about it?
- What problems or challenges does it face?
- What's its most recent triumph or disaster?
- Who makes which decisions?

Now, let's take each of these sample questions separately:

How's the Company Doing?

No company is ever in a truly neutral position. It may be doing badly. It may be growing apace. It may be in much the same position as last year, which, in many cases, means it's doing badly but that its problems are not yet acute. How it's doing will seriously influence the attitude of any potential purchaser within the organisation to buying your product or service. It may also make that product or service more or less relevant or topical.

How Is It Managed?

Not so long ago, someone who shall be nameless (because he's well known) had a meeting with Michael O'Leary of Ryanair to seek sponsorship from him for a project the nameless person planned.

Mr Nameless was agreeably surprised by how briskly pleasant O'Leary was.

'Would you like a Coke?' the Ryanair man asked. Mr Nameless allowed as how that would be most welcome. O'Leary strode to a Coke vending machine in the corner, released a can from it, dropped it on the table in front of Mr Nameless and held out his hand, palm upward.

'That'll be two Euro,' he announced.

Mr Nameless paid up, adding this nugget of behaviour to what he already knew about Michael O'Leary. He had researched the man by going through newspaper cuttings and DVDs provided by his PR company and reading a paperback book about the tartan-shirted tycoon. He knew, for example, that O'Leary's cost-control was legendary but the Coke for which he had to pay reinforced this information. Mr Nameless, accordingly, made a pitch different in tone, pace, content and length from what he had made to any other captain of industry.

Any salesperson needs a real sense, long before they make the first call, of how a company is managed and what the priorities of its lead team are. Finding out this information can be easy (as in the case of Michael O'Leary, a media darling whose philosophy is played out in public every second day) or hard (as in the case of older family-run firms, which don't seek personal publicity and put as little information as possible on their website other than where to find them and buy whatever they offer.)

To find out about the theory and the practice within your target companies, use your contacts. As we've noted about Ireland, most of us can find links to people within a few steps. Talk first to the people you know who actually know the firm. Ask what their impression is, who the key people are, what they know about their the company's situation and prospects, who their suppliers are and any other little details they might have.

Some of these details may send you screaming in the opposite direction. For example, you may learn that they don't pay their bills, that their CEO is barking and that their HR practices are soul-destroying. Just as you have a set of ethical standards for target companies to meet, you also need a clear idea of what other attributes you desire – and which traits will rule potential client companies out fast. Try to develop a sense of these in advance and not as a result of bitter experience.

What's Special, New or Different about the Company?

You may not think that Company X is special but the chances are that at least some of the people – starting at ownership and management level – think it's very special. If they do and if you want to sell something to them, now and in the long-term, you'd better identify what they consider special about themselves.

Here's an example. One major multi-national devotes time and energy, every year, to its recruitment process. It attends university job fairs, puts advertisements in the papers and sets out to find the brightest and best of that year's graduate crop. It conducts rigorous interviews. And, every now and then, some bright graduate falls at the last fence. You know that moment when the prospective employer asks the interviewee if there's any question they'd like to put to the interview board before the interview concludes? Some candidates kill their chances at that point by asking a simple, obvious and – to the applicant – pivotally important question: 'What would I be paid?' they ask. (Or the posher version: 'Could you indicate the compensation package?')

The interview panel makes noncommittal noises, thanks the applicant warmly, delivers firm handshakes and the candidate has no clue that they have just shot themselves, not in the foot, but in the heart. This particular company prides itself on taking care of its employees and paying over the odds, and if an applicant doesn't know that and trust them to pay well, they want no part of that applicant, no matter how superb his or her academic record. In this instance, failure to do the necessary research cripples applicants' chances of selling themselves.

In the more general sales area, I recently sat in on a series of pitches being made by individuals who wanted to get on to the preferred-supplier list of a medium-sized company. In the debrief after the presentations, I was surprised to find one potential supplier ruled out without discussion. When I queried their removal, the managing director laughed and explained:

> The guy kept saying 'companies like yours'. He kept telling us about work he'd done for similar companies. He never even mentioned the name of our company. To him, we're just a sausage on an assembly line. We long ago made a rule that the minute anybody says 'companies like yours', they're dead. There are no companies like ours. There are companies in the same sector. There are competitor companies. But they're not us and we're not them and if he can't distinguish us from all the others, we don't want to know him.

People hate to be treated as a cross-section of manufacturing or as a slice of a demographic. They see themselves and their company as unique and if you want to sell to them, you must do likewise.

Nor do companies have to be long-established household names before they develop this sense of personal brand. New companies develop it very quickly and the more pronounced their sense of differentiation, the more successful they're likely to be in a downturn. Copycats do nicely in boom times. They do markedly less well in recessionary times.

When you research a start-up company or a relatively new venture, you will quickly find that, in information terms, their bottoms are clean. Nothing to do with personal hygiene. Everything to do with corporate history. Companies in business a long time tend to be encrusted with accessible history, the way the underside of a ship is encrusted with barnacles. Even the most secretive companies leak information in the form of newspaper photographs of founders, details of wills, news reports of key personnel getting married, graduating or being done for drunk driving. Less secretive companies appear before the public gaze for winning awards and a multiplicity of other reasons.

Just as the bottom of a newly-launched ship is clean of barnacles, a newer company may have few accretions, in terms of easily got-at information. But this doesn't mean that the owners are not networked and known. Banks know them. People who went to school or college or played sports with them know them. Enterprise Ireland or other state bodies may know them. Back when they first saw an opening in the market, they talked to friends or acquaintances about the possibilities for the business. You need to find people who have interfaced with the company or the individuals within the company. Just ask around, starting with the more connected people of your acquaintance. Sooner than you expect, someone will say, 'Oh, your man? His mother and my mother were in Carysfort [the teacher training college] together.' Or 'Well, I've never met him but his sister did a line with my best man and they stayed friends even when they broke up.'

With every contact you make, avoid asking straightforward questions, the answers to which are freely available on websites, media sites and through organisations like the Companies Registration Office (CRO). You want insider trading. You want insight. You want flavour. You want to know what makes the people who work for this particular company tick, whether they tick in unison and who in the company has the loudest tick.

Sometimes, even a throwaway comment about an individual can be useful. Years ago, I asked a man about someone who I believed should be buying our services. He gave me lots of information I already had. I wrote it all down again and expressed my gratitude.

'Now, sum up his personality for me,' I said.

He stopped. Thought about it. And began to laugh. 'He's the sort of guy who would have all his hangers pointing the same way.'

This insight was worth more than volumes of objective data to me.

Sometimes, the information you dig out will seem contradictory. Keep writing it down. You can analyse it later. Here's an example of an ostensible contradiction that, in fact, revealed a great deal about the values of the purchasing organisation.

At one point in my career, when I headed up a non-governmental organisation, one of our suppliers sold a particular brand of coffee. They found it difficult to understand why I preferred a more expensive brand.

'The thing is, you're a charity and this is the cheapest brand,' the sales rep said, one day. 'That's the only reason I suggested it.'

The minute he'd said it, he realised I might take a huff

at the suggestion I was spending more (donated) money than I needed to, out of personal preference, and tried to take back his comment. I laughed and explained that the cheaper company had a record of dumping baby milk powder on third world countries in a way that undermined breastfeeding and led directly to an increase in infant deaths in these countries. Up to then he had a superficial understanding of our sector (they don't have much money – they're a charity). After we talked, he understood that charities, especially children's charities, have a principled approach to purchases. And, because he was a very good salesman, I have no doubt that this changed the way he dealt with other non-profit organisations from then on.

Nowadays many companies see the benefit, ecological and financial, of an open, ethical values system. If you want to sell to them, you must consider this. A while ago, an organisation made their awarding of a tender to my company, the Communications Clinic, contingent on our meeting certain waste management criteria – and went so far as to inspect out premises to confirm our assurances.

How can you be sure about a company's or organisation's values? Mostly, you'd hope, they will be manifest in their behaviours, although this is not always the case. Now and again, you'll come across an organisation that claims to be environmentally friendly but when you look a little closer, you'll find it doesn't deliver on the claim. The staff don't reuse or recycle and they certainly don't actively seek to reduce their carbon emissions. In straitened times, short-sightedness often leads to cheaper purchases, that do long-term damage not just to the environment but to the reputation of the firm itself.

If at all possible, get an introduction to someone in the company who'd be prepared to talk to you to help you in your fact-finding quest. If you decide to target this company, you'll be trying to identify someone who'll give you fairly objective information and maybe become your in-house champion farther down the line. By this I mean someone senior enough to influence buying decisions and with whom you'll be able to form a good relationship. But for now, you just need to talk to someone who can give you accurate information.

If you can't get an introduction, talk to the person who habitually answers the phone. Explain that you're simply ringing for information about the firm – leave the key personnel out of it at the beginning – and they'll probably tell you a great deal, even if they think they aren't divulging anything significant. Take notes.

For example, you may ring up a firm of lawyers. The big firms have well-trained people staffing the phones who'll always be friendly and professional. They will give you quite a bit of general information and also more details about who does what in the firm, especially if any changes have recently taken place. They may also tell you who's currently out at lunch, who makes buying decisions about various products and services and what your chances are of talking to one of the most senior partners. Take notes.

You notice I keep recommending taking notes. Recording what you learn about companies and organisations is imperative. You think you'll remember what Philip said about his boss and you may – for a few days. Your aim, though, is to build up a comprehensive knowledge of your target industry and businesses. Are you going to be able to keep it all in your head? And if, God forbid, you broke a leg, where would any member of your company find your valuable information while you're recuperating?

Keep every piece of data on file. When you meet people for coffee or talk to them on the phone you'll probably make hand-written notes. You should transfer them to clearly annotated pages that same day and preferably as soon as the call is over. You'll remember a depth of detail right then that you'll have forgotten even the next day. That crucial detail which you might not immediately consider relevant (say, that Philip's boss gets hot and bothered over Dublin traffic) could make all the difference in establishing rapport in your initial meeting with this same boss. So write everything down, even if it doesn't seem germane.

Then transfer your notes to a database. Please, transfer them to a database. Unless you've spent three hours fruitlessly looking for a vital phone number, you have no idea how critical this is. The situation is so much worse when all you can remember is a first name – no surname, no company name. It's a disaster. An easily avoided disaster. Paper is destructible and dead easy to lose. Put as much information as possible into your database, then back it up.

Just make sure that it's information that doesn't breach the Data Protection regulations. It would not be legitimate, for example, for your hard disc to contain gossip about the marketing manager of a particular company that suggests that he has an active extracurricular sex life. It would be quite appropriate to record the fact that the charity I mentioned earlier has a rigorously ethical approach to purchases but not to describe a prospective customer as the kind of guy who has all his hangers pointing in the same direction. Keep gossip and personal judgement out of what you store in your database. Keep in mind the worst-case scenario that for some reason your database is read out in court. It shouldn't have anything in it that will shame you, get you fired or cause you to be sued or fined.

A coherent database allows you to access not just contact details but the notes you took and any information other people gave you about your contact. And you can add every extra piece of useful data, quickly and easily, as you get it.

Which Threats or Challenges Does the Target Company Face?
Threats and challenges can be immediate, medium-term or long-term.

An immediate threat might be action on the part of the Environmental Protection Agency as a result of a toxic leak or emission. It might be constrained cashflow.

A mid-term threat might be a new product. The iPhone presents a profound mid-term threat to the BlackBerry, for example.

A long-term threat to the local branch of a multi-national manufacturing company might be a change in policy within HQ to move all manufacturing to China within five years, as a result of China's tendency to allow companies that provide employment within China to trade within its borders.

Understanding the opportunities and threats facing a company gives you a special insight into that company – essential, if you're going to sell to that company. But don't get into decision-making too soon. Before you find your prince – your ideal buying company – you may have to kiss a lot of frogs.

In relationship selling in Ireland, you need to rely on your friends, acquaintances and business contacts, because the word gets round so fast here. People love to be asked for their advice and they may be a bit put out if you don't ask them. For example, your friend Bernie is PA to the CEO of a company you don't see as being directly in the market for what you have to sell. Yes, the company is a potential customer but you think companies X, Y and Z are more suitable prospects. So you try to build up contacts in each of those companies because they're likely to need your offering right away.

Ireland is a small place and Bernie hears about your enquiries. A few things strike her. Firstly, why didn't you ask her advice? She could have warned you off that wagon, Esther, in Company Z and she actually knows John, in Company X, quite well. He and she have helped each other out from time to time and she knows he's sound. Secondly, if you didn't feel able to talk to her, something must be wrong in your company. You wouldn't have been able to hide it from her – you're such good friends – so you didn't feel able to talk to her. Finally she wonders: maybe you're not quite such good friends as she had thought.

See what you did? You missed out on good steers, you raised unnecessary doubts and you damaged a valuable relationship. Never miss the opportunity to talk to someone you know in search of contacts.

You may be thinking: I can't give away all my plans to Bernie. Bernie, like all of us, is more concerned with herself and her work and life than with you and yours. So when you ask for a contact in Company X, she's unlikely to get on Facebook to let the world know. Besides, Bernie is not stupid. She knows you have to build up prospects and you may be a useful contact for someone she knows, like John in Company X. That's what you need – willing helpers. You get them only through using your relationships.

By the same token, you should be a helper. If you hear or observe that Pamela in Company W has just been promoted and realise that this would be useful information for Bernie or her boss, make sure you phone or email Bernie – soon. It's especially helpful to get important news to someone fast. In relationship selling that's your goal – helpfulness. So practise it all the time.

If you have the good sense to check with all your Bernies – all those people you know in companies up and down the country – for help in developing prospect contacts, you'll unearth useful information. For instance, they'll let you know what not to waste your time on: organisations heading for examinership or receivership (unless you're in accountancy or law, in which case these might be entities to contact) or those embroiled in major buy-outs or internal reorganisation (unless you're in management consultancy). They'll alert you to changes in personnel and may be able to advise you on who the real decision-makers are.

What's the Company's Most Recent Triumph or Disaster?
If, just last week, the CEO was beaten bloody by Vincent Brown on TV3's late-night show, or if, just a fortnight ago, the company won an international award, you can look like a complete plonker if you don't know about this disaster or triumph.

Who Makes Which Decisions?

In the organisation chart, it looks simple and clear. In the real world, the chart may have little or no relation to reality. The person who is head of marketing may ostensibly make the decision to buy an advertising campaign but it may be the chief financial officer who has the final, vital say. The fact that someone has a title can, in one company, mean that they make the significant purchasing decisions, while in another company this may not be the case at all. Joe Nobody may have the title of 'training manager' but in fact may be little more than PA to the HR manager in their company, while it is the HR Manager who places people on training programmes. In some team-led Irish branches of multi-national companies, the person who is titular head of, say, quality control may, in fact, be the person who most influences purchases of new technology or furniture.

When you undertake the research stage – the first stage of any strategic sale – developing a sense of who makes which decisions in a company and who buys what is a high priority, which, if neglected, can result in the situation, sadly familiar to many salespeople, where they get through all the gates, get in front of the person with the relevant title, make their pitch to huge enthusiasm from that person, yet never receive an order or a confirmation of a sale, because that person either doesn't have real buying power or prefers not to exercise the power they have.

This is where having an internal champion is vital. A champion is someone who knows, likes and values you, your product or service or perhaps your company, and marks your card on how to manage the internal dynamics within their company. Card-marking can take one or more of a number of forms. A champion may tell you, for example, that the PA to the CEO is the key buying influence. She may not appear on any website or organisational chart. She may never figure in an annual report. But she is the person who does the grunt work on any major purchase and you disregard her at your peril. Or a champion may fill you in on the business gurus who influence the thinking of the key buying influence. Or warn you about a bad experience the key buying influence had with another company selling your kind of product or service.

Champions don't have to be highly placed within an organisation. It helps if they're at a level where, should they put in a good word for you, that good word will register where it counts. But sometimes, they're to be found at lower levels. Their value to you resides in them being the kind of people who understand what's really going on in their company and the hot buttons that need to be pressed when you're in contact with particular individuals. Indeed, some champions are to be found outside a company. Take, for example, a CEO who retains an external advisor or mentor who greatly influences their thinking. In this situation, the external figure can be your champion.

When dealing with a champion, keep three things in mind:

- Keep it ethical. It's OK for an internal person to advise an external supplier, as long as the outcome is beneficial to their own company. The internal champion who is prepared to do more than card-marking – who will push the interests of that supplier at the expense of someone whose offering is better for their own company – is unethical and dangerous. The internal champion who takes backhanders from an external supplier is unethical and treacherous.

- Keep it clean. Don't ask for advice or help that you know goes beyond the point of decency and don't *ever* pay for advice or information. The champion you want will derive their reward from saving their own company time by cutting away irrelevant undergrowth from your approach to that company and from the pleasure of being consulted. No more. No less.

- Salespeople promoting a good product or service who stay connected with customers often find that a contact from one company who moves to another will spontaneously suggest that you approach someone in the new company with a specific offering that they know will be of value to their new employer. Now, that's a real champion…

HOW WELL DO I KNOW
THE TARGET COMPANY?

Which industry are they in? ....
....

What is their core business? ....
....

How big/small is the company? ....
....

Who are their main customers? ....
....

How has the business changed in the past year?
....
....

What is its current biggest industry/business
challenge? ....
....

Who is their biggest competitor? ....
....

How is the competitor doing compared with the target company in the key areas? ....

....

Who is the target company CEO? What's s/he like?

....

....

Who is the CFO? What's s/he like? ....

....

....

Who is our internal contact? His or her role in the company? ....

....

Have we pitched to them before? ....
When? ....

With what outcome? ....

....

Who from our side was involved? ....

....

....

If no sale, why? ....

....

Have we sold to them before? ....

If yes, what? ....

How did we add value? ....
....

What feedback did we get? ....
....

Who is our company's closest contact with them?
....

For this sale, who is the decision-maker? ....
....

What's the latest on the grapevine? ....
....
....

When was our last contact with them? ....

What was the nature of the contact? ....
....
....

Other issues of importance ....
....
....

4

COLD CALLING

Cold calling is the second stage in a five-stage strategic selling process. It's also the one which strikes most terror into salespeople, whose insides go into locked rigidity at the very thought of lifting the phone and seeking an appointment with the key buying influence.

COUNTERPRODUCTIVE BEHAVIOURS
Fear of personal rejection is a shrivelling reality which comes into play at this point with such force that it drives salespeople into a series of counterproductive behaviours, including:

Postponement
The salesperson convinces themselves that more research must be done before they actually approach an individual or a company.

Playacting
This can take different forms. One is making calls but putting down the phone before it's answered and logging the failed calls as if they were worthwhile activity. Another is sending a letter seeking an appointment and then

leaving it to the prospect to get back to the salesperson. A third is adopting a false 'self.' This last one happens when the salesperson copies another sales rep or picks a method out of a book, so they ring the prospect and say something like, 'I could save your company thousands in one day and make you a hero within your management team.'

One marketing manager recently contacted me about a fourth version of playacting which was new to him and to me. His salesforce operated in cubicles surrounding his workspace, so he could, when it suited him, overhear their calls. He told me:

> Nine times out of ten, I take no action after I hear a cold call being made. That's because the call is being done according to instructions. Nine times out of ten, when I do take action, it's to tell the sales rep that they're doing a particularly good job. I stand near where they sit and talk to them about a neat approach I've heard them take. That way, their colleagues get to learn from what they've done right. Very rarely, when I hear a rep saying something counterproductive, I'll catch them in a corridor later, where nobody can witness what passes between us, and suggest a better alternative to what they're doing.

So far, so good. Except that, a few weeks earlier, he had become aware that a new salesman was disappearing for hours at a time into a breakout room more commonly used for client meetings. He accosted the salesperson and indicated that if the salesperson was that shy, he wasn't in the right job. Cold calling was to be done from the salesperson's desk. Clear? Clear.

> I was very impressed, in the following couple of weeks, by the calls I heard him make. They were really good. I just couldn't figure why his schedule didn't show more company visits by way of follow-up.

On impulse, the marketing manager checked the employee's telephone records and was startled to find what they revealed. The first revelation was that, in about four out of ten of outgoing calls, the sales rep was diverting the call directly into voicemail. They were, in other words, deliberately avoiding direct contact with the person with whom, on the face of it, they were trying to establish a relationship. The second thing he discovered was that in at least five out of ten calls, the salesman was dialling the number, then cutting off the connection and talking into a dead phone. Only one in ten calls was being made to a real person in real time.

Most marketing managers would have canned the sales rep involved immediately but this man decided to give the guy another chance: 'I figure he has a lot of brainpower, to have worked out such clever ways of not doing the job and if I can capture and redirect that brainpower, I might have a hell of an operator on my hands.'

Phoning to Fail
Phoning to fail works this way. The salesperson reaches the potential customer and instead of genuinely seeking

a meeting, gives the potential customer several ways in which to avoid having such a meeting:

'Michael, I know you currently have a gizmo supplier and you're probably very happy with them but I really would love to come and talk to you about our gizmos. I suppose you're very busy?'

I trained one man who had brought phoning to fail to a fine art. He belonged in *The Guinness Book of Records* for his capacity to hide his light under a bushel. He would never tell the person he reached what precisely his product was, implying that if the person had their wits about them, they would meet him (of whom they'd never heard) urgently (he always wanted to see them the next day) in order to be rescued (from some non-specific threat) by his brilliant but secret offering. Understandably, his calls met with zero success.

Now, let's address four common misunderstandings about cold-calling that lead intelligent people into such strange ways of avoiding them.

YOU JUST LIFT THE PHONE

No, you don't. It's a lot easier to cross a river by a bridge than to try to leap it: starting a relationship with a prospective client with a telephone call out of the blue from someone of whom they've never heard is the equivalent of trying to cross the Shannon at one bound. Try finding stepping stones or erecting a bridge, first.

Once, as outlined in the previous chapter, you have identified the key buying influence, you work out how to lay down a bridge to them. An introduction is ideal. People love making introductions as long as they trust the person and product they're introducing. It doesn't take a huge amount of time to make a phone call to a friend saying, 'Look, I've had great work done for me by Rose Cullen of the Safety Network. If she rings you, would you give her five minutes?'

Permission to quote someone's name can also provide a plank in a bridge to the person you want to reach. Reaching their personal assistant is another method, even if it's only to get the target person's email address and flag the assistant that you're going to send a letter seeking an appointment. If the assistant, or, in some cases, the receptionist, asks why you want the email address, explain who you are, to which company or organisation you belong and that you wish to send a letter. If they offer extra information – and they usually do, if only to head off unwanted callers from their boss – accept it happily and ask more questions. Remember that it's never too early to start making relationships. Above all, don't get loftily huffy. A colleague of mine, who was told by the secretary to the managing partner in a legal firm that equipment purchasing never goes as high as partner level, still insisted that this was where her letter was going. In this way she cut herself off from further information she might have found useful and simultaneously put the secretary's back up. That particular contact went exactly nowhere.

YOU SHOULD START BY SENDING A PROSPECTUS OR BROCHURE

No you shouldn't. The first point about glossy promotional literature is that most busy people don't read it. Some of them have positive intentions and put it in their in box but several CEOs with whom I have worked had a standing instruction to their assistants: trade magazines, annual reports, leaflets and brochures were never to be left on their desk. Someone else was to read them, if they believed the task was worth the candle. Should they find something in a publication meriting the CEO's attention, they should cut it out and send it on.

The second point about glossy promotional literature is that, unless it's outstandingly and eye-catchingly presented, it won't get a second glance at any level within the organisation because it is so clearly aimed at everybody in the world, rather than carefully crafted to scratch the itch of any individual.

YOU SHOULD SAVE TIME BY PUTTING THE KEY SELLING MESSAGES IN YOUR INTRODUCTORY LETTER

That's to miss the purpose of a cold call letter. The purpose of writing the letter is to sell a phone-call, to sell a meeting or to find out more information about the target company. It's much too soon to be pitching.

YOU LEAVE IT UP TO THEM TO RESPOND

You're the one with something to sell. Why should they do their job for you? 'Please do not hesitate to call me,' should never be included in any letter for any purpose at any time. In a cold call letter, it's a disqualifier. Instead, indicate when you'll ring to seek a brief meeting.

YOU SEND THE SAME LETTER TO HUNDREDS OF COMPANIES IN THE SAME SECTOR

This emerges from the old 'mud on the wall' approach to marketing, which holds that if you slap enough mud on a wall, some of it will stick and, extrapolating from mud-adhesion, if you slap enough letters on enough desks, one or two of them will result in a sale. Possibly – if what you're flogging is a cheap new gadget. In that instance, for argument's sake, one of your letters may land on the desk of someone who, in an idle moment, may yield to the impulse to buy a clock that projects the time onto the ceiling. But remember, a strategic sale is different. A strategic sale demands that the purchaser spend a significant amount of company money, rather than back-pocket cash. It involves some change in work by staff, either in the installation of the product or system or in its ongoing use. The authorisation of its purchase is likely to involve more than one person; even if the final decision rests with an individual, this individual will listen to input from others.

For all these reasons, a strategic sale is a relationship sale. Learning about the company and the person in question was the objective of doing the research in the first stage of the sale. Getting to know and be known by the potential customer is the purpose of cold-calling, the second stage of the sale. A generic letter runs counter to that intention.

Communications expert Tom Savage maintains that in every contact with customers, you are either *building* or *unbuilding* a relationship. Sending an email or a snail mail letter that yellow-packs the recipient is one sure way to unbuild a relationship. Instead, when writing the letter to sell a telephone call, begin by introducing yourself and your company or organisation. But that's all. This should be brief. The person who is going to receive the letter doesn't want to read reams about you or the company. Get to the nub of your communication quickly.

The first paragraph – indeed, the first sentence – is where any mention of the recommendation by a mutual friend or contact goes.

The next paragraph is critical. Here's where you give a good reason (from the recipient's point of view) for meeting you. The reason must be cogent. It must be to remove or minimise a threat, to confer a real business or personal benefit or to pass on something of business interest. Research shows that people pay attention first to what threatens them, next to what benefits them and finally to something of interest.

Your letter should indicate some understanding of the recipient's organisation but should also make clear that the meeting you seek is for information only. You think you may have something that would interest them but you promise you're not going to arrive in their office and try to flog them something. You're genuinely seeking information. Again, this should be brief – if possible, no longer than a single sentence. Then mention that you'll be following up with a call to fix a date and time for the meeting. Type your name at the bottom but leave space for your handwritten signature, if it's a letter to be delivered by An Post. Consider adding a handwritten postscript. Anything that makes a letter more personal, less formulaic, helps it to stand out from the others landing on the recipient's desk every day of the week.

Even at this point, your research may allow you to create real links with the recipient of your letter, not by evincing an inappropriate over-familiarity but by responding to their revealed preferences. Above all, get the name and title correct. You can't afford, for example, to assume that someone with a unisex name like Hilary is a woman just because you associate the name with Hillary Clinton. You can't afford to assume that every woman in the chair of a board refers to themselves as a chairperson. Gillian Bowler, who chairs Irish Life and Permanent, prefers to use the term 'Chairman' to describe her role. You can't afford to spell someone's name the way you're used to spelling it. Rory is not Ruairí and it sure as hell is not Ruaidhrí. Getting someone's name or title wrong puts a disproportionately sizeable obstacle in the way of relationship-building. People's names matter to them and failure to pay attention to names is inimical to good salesmanship.

The next task in this second stage of the five-stage selling process is making the follow-up call. These are the things to watch:

- Always make the call yourself – don't delegate. Remember that you're building a relationship. You can't get to know somebody by avoiding an vital early encounter with them.
- The higher the person is in the company, the earlier they're likely to be at work and the greater the possibility that they will be open to your request, because they're likely to have their electronic diary readily accessible and not be surrounded by colleagues.
- Ask for the person you've written to by their formal name.
- Give your name and your company's name and your role in the company – briefly but clearly.

- Explain to the secretary or personal assistant that you are following up on a letter sent the previous week.
- If you're asked, give the reason (as already outlined in your letter) for wanting the meeting, stressing that it's not a sales call.
- If your target person is not available or busy, don't put down the phone. Leave a cheerful greeting, a brief message and a clearly articulated phone number, repeated at dictation pace. Then add that you'll call back and give some indication of the time. If you reach an assistant or a colleague, ask what the best time is – in their experience – to telephone the person you want to reach.
- Keep control of the process. In other words, if an assistant offers to put you on to someone else, or to get someone else to call you, be properly grateful and willing to talk to that other person but make it clear that it's someone else you really want to reach and that you will ring this person again.
- Be open, friendly and positive with the person who takes your call, whatever the outcome.

When you get to talk to your prospect, your task is to move the process to the third stage – confirming the meeting. Introduce yourself and your company and explain why you want the meeting. Be clear that you're looking for a meeting because you have something to offer that is of benefit to the prospect but that you aren't going to waste their time offering something unless you can be sure it will be helpful to them. Don't make the fatal mistake of offering a product at this time. You want to establish the benefits of clarifying the precise needs of the targeted company and of your prospect.

Prepare in advance so you can make the phone call productive. The encounter is going to be in the spoken word, so you should prepare in the spoken word. You don't need a script but you do need to have heard yourself go through the encounter before it actually happens, working out your best response to likely responses. Preparing in the spoken word eliminates nervous burbles, like the salesperson a well-known managing director told me about recently. Because the MD is a direct, no-messing person who doesn't see the need to be surrounded by a phalanx of subordinates dedicated to preventing people from reaching him, when the caller asked to talk to him, she was put through and he picked up the phone.

'Oh, you're not serious?' was her interrogative greeting. 'It's really you? I wouldn't – I mean I never expected you to answer yourself, pick up the phone, you know? Omigod, I'm sorry but I'm totally unnerved.'

That caller was making the fundamental error of the under-prepared salesperson. She was focused on her own needs, reactions and emotions, rather than on those of the person she wanted as a customer. When you're preparing to sell – whether you're selling a product, a service or yourself in a job interview, smack yourself upside the head whenever you hear yourself expressing a personal opinion, desire, feeling or need. It's like the old advice about teaching a pig to sing: it wastes your time and irritates the pig. Talking about yourself wastes time and irritates the person you who is on the other end of the line. Irish people do it all the time without realising who is the subject of the conversation.

'I have to tell you, I'm your biggest fan,' they'll say to a prospect. 'I always wanted to work in aviation myself. I'd probably have become a pilot if it wasn't for my eyesight being so bad. It was my father who used to talk about you, really, but then...'

The person doing the talking may believe she's talking about the other guy but her guff is boomerang-shaped. Good salespeople never do boomerang conversation. They are obsessive about their interest in and focus on the other person. They keep their need to talk, their opinions and their desire to argue out of their work, concentrating, instead, on finding the other person interesting.

Preparing out loud for a phone call may seem excessive and after some time in the selling business you may be able to dispense with it. But in the early days, it allows you to reality-test an encounter on which all of the other steps of the selling process are predicated.

When you get to the real phone call:

- First of all, be warm but be authentic. Most of us smile as we talk to a friend but because we can't see the recipient of our phone call in front of us, we forget to smile when we're talking to them on the phone. Bring your strengths to a cold call. Present the best version of yourself. Don't go into official, fast-talking cold-call mode and iron yourself flat in the process.

- Remember that while your primary objective is to set up a meeting with the prospective client, you are still in the research stage of the sale. Listen, not just to what the other person says but to *how* they say it. People leak information about themselves, their priorities and their preferences in virtually every encounter. Capture any leaks and write them down. Even paying attention to the language the other person uses will help you know them a little better at the end of the phone call.
- Describe yourself and your company and explain why you want the meeting.
- State the benefits of being able to establish the precise needs of the targeted company and of meeting the person in question.
- Make it clear the meeting would only be for fifteen minutes.
- Don't cast yourself as a plaintive subservient. You believe you have a commonality of interest with the person with whom you're talking. You believe there's a good chance what you'll eventually sell them will be good for their bottom line. (If you don't believe it would be useful to them, get into another job, because trying to sell costly unnecessary items to others is one of the most personally destructive jobs in the world.) Plaintive subservient includes things like, 'I know you're in constant demand and that you must

be terribly busy but I would be really, really grateful if you could spare me ten minutes of your valuable time.' This is the Uriah Heep style of cold-calling and it rarely works. 'What's the best day for you?' is the kind of question a colleague or a friend asks. It's the kind of question someone who respects themselves asks. Ask it. Or suggest a date for meeting: 'Would Friday suit?' or, 'How about some day the following week?'

- When a date has been agreed, suggest a time like 11:15 or 2:45 (don't go on the hour) as this confirms to your host that you mean what you say about taking up only fifteen minutes of their time.
- Don't discuss your product or service in detail on the phone. Even if you're asked. Find an unpompous way to get out of it: 'Listen, you're in danger of getting me started on stuff I love that might be of no interest to you. How about I drop in to your office for fifteen minutes early next week so I don't waste your time on the phone?'
- Don't send literature in advance.
- Get off the phone quickly once you have confirmed the day, date and time of the meeting.

KEY OUTCOMES FROM THE COLD CALL

1. What have you learned about the industry/ business you didn't know before? ....
....

2. Who are key company personnel?

    a. Influencers? ....

    b. Decision-makers? ....

    c. Technical influencers? ....

    d. User influencers? ....

3. What current challenges face the company? ....
....

4. How can you help, or do you need more information? ....
....

5. If you need more information, list in detail what else you need to know? ....
....
....
....

6. What next steps have been agreed? ....

....

....

7. What else could you do, over and above these
steps, to build the relationship? ....

....

....

8. Who should you talk to in your own company? ....

....

....

9. What do you need to ask them? ....

....

....

10. Modify approach? ....

....

11. Timeline and achievement indicators for new
approach ....

....

12. Any other information/insight? ....

....

....

......

5

THE FIRST MEETING:
WATCHING, ASKING, LISTENING

The third stage of the strategic sales process is the meeting you've set up with the relevant executive in the company to which you sell. When you have organised the first meeting, be aware that it doesn't start when you're ushered into the office of the man or woman who has agreed to talk to you. Arrive with plenty of time to spare and start your research in the car park.

Unrealistic? Not at all. A car park yields up an enormous amount of information. It may have meeting-place signs related to evacuation in the event of a crisis. It may have special named slots for VIPs within management. It may be potholed and littered or beautifully taken care of. Just as you can learn a great deal about a family from looking at their front garden, if they have one (including the age of the owners, the age of their children and the priority given to cars in the household), you can learn a lot about an organisation from its car park.

One saleswoman I trained rang me, a few months after a course she had done with the Communications Clinic, to tell me about her biggest sale to date:

I was in the car park early, following instructions, so there weren't that many other cars parked and I could see that the only named space belonged to the managing director. Just as I was about to turn off *Morning Ireland* and go to the lobby, a Nissan Micra pulled into the MD's space and a young woman opened the door, pulled a wheelchair from behind the passenger seat, got into it and disappeared into the offices. A few minutes later, when I was waiting at Reception, I said to the receptionist that I hadn't known their MD was in a wheelchair. She laughed and said he wasn't but that a few weeks earlier, he'd arrived in a bit late, swanned into his slot and then noticed the Micra driver struggling to park her car in a difficult corner in such a way as to allow her to get out of it and into the wheelchair. The managing director, who was only a few weeks in the job, marched into Reception and instructed that from now on, his spot should belong to the Micra driver, whose name was Dorothy. They hadn't got around to marking it with the wheelchair sign but the word had gone out like lightning among the staff, so everybody knew.

Just having found out this little bit of information changed the entire sales process, because I went into my meeting liking the company more and with a much more positive attitude. The sale took several meetings but

> eventually came through. I've had to be in
> and out of the company a lot, so I made it my
> business to seek out Dorothy and tell her how
> helpful her parking in the MD's slot was to me.

In the lobby, just as in the car park, you will find information that you can use as a conversation-starter or – later on – as a way of informing the proposal document you write to the company. And I don't just mean visual information. I once overheard two staff members in the reception area of their own company sharing unofficial information about company plans to move some of the manufacturing lines to India. I'd been asked to meet with the board of the company about an unspecified 'emerging issue.' When I was brought into the boardroom, I took an educated risk.

'So, Chairman,' I said, accepting a cup of coffee from him. 'You need to work out how to achieve local buy-in to the shift of the two manufacturing lines to Bangalore?'

I was lucky the cup and saucer had changed hands, because if I'd shot him I couldn't have evoked a better startle response. The entire room vibrated in silence as board members looked at me in horror. This was an industrial secret which could have a major impact on their share price if its communication was not tightly managed and here was this consultant – a total stranger to them – who had rumbled it from the start.

I protected my sources but had a much more productive meeting as a result of the remarks I'd overheard because the board now understood the importance of the corporate grapevine.

Any reference you make to something you've observed about the company prior to the meeting can be an ice-breaker and obviate the need to make small-talk about the weather. But don't waste time on peripherals. Remember to stick to your promise to take no more than fifteen minutes of the relevant person's time. Or thirty. Or ten. Trust begins with your keeping your word, so make sure you keep your word about the duration of the meeting. If the other person pooh-poohs the timing and is happy to talk, of course you can stay longer but be very sure that the invitation is genuine rather than merely courteous.

You're there to listen so you should use no more than 20 per cent of those fifteen minutes in asking questions. That's three minutes. So your questions must be good. And your listening must be great.

The Trusted Advisor by British consultant, David Maister, is a book every salesperson should read. It hammers home the fact that how you listen is crucial.

'As you listen to a client talk,' Maister says, 'the question on your mind should be, 'What makes this person different from any other client I've served? What does that mean for what I should say and how I should behave?''

Maister admits it's hard work to do as he advises, not least because we instinctively do the opposite. Either we talk rather than listen or, when we listen, we're on the aural hunt for themes and topics we recognise and are comfortable with. Maister's main point is that it is only by listening for what you don't already know and are not comfortably familiar with that you can get to the right position with a prospective purchaser or client.

'Before you can help someone, you need to understand

what's on their mind,' he stresses. 'You must create situations where they will tell you more about their issues, concerns and needs.'

Getting to know people's issues, concerns and needs will depend not just on how you listen but on the questions you ask and how you ask them. For this initial meeting make two lists: one based on what you need to know and the other based on what you think would indicate a good understanding of their industry, company and their individual issues.

Let's say you want to know:

- What the company's training needs are
- What budget is assigned to training
- Who usually does training for them

The list of what you think would indicate an understanding of the company and its business might include:

- How the company is faring in the downturn
- What the downturn means for the company – having to let people go, seeking new investors?
- The company's emphasis on quality customer service
- The company's reliance on public tenders for a good part of their business

Be very clear. You should not go into this first exploratory meeting carrying lists of questions, any more than a broadcaster should go into a programme with a list of questions to ask the programme's guests. Lists create loyalties and, if you're nervous, you may find yourself following the sequence too faithfully, which tends to have a number of negative outcomes, not least of which may be irritation on the part of the person you're interviewing at being so obviously subjected to a process. Nobody ever wants to be part of a process.

The other downside of bringing a list of questions into a sales encounter is that it interferes with your capacity to listen. You may miss something as you plough relentlessly through each query. By all means bring notes so that you don't forget anything but keep them at the back of your notebook or clipboard. That way, towards the end of the meeting, you can glance at them in order to ensure that you haven't missed anything: in this way they will not have become a barrier between the other person and you.

Unless you have shorthand and almost nobody does any more, you will need to record the meeting. Be so familiar with your recording device that it fits seamlessly into the developing relationship and present it casually to the person you are meeting as a way to ensure you don't lose any of the valuable insights he or she may share with you. Doing six sound checks, messing with leads or discovering you are low on battery power are the marks of an amateur. An incompetent amateur who does not value the time they've been given.

Once your recording device is up and running, it's time to ask questions. Or, rather, it's time to get the other person talking. They're not always the same thing. Sometimes, people ask questions in order to be impressive. When your goal is to find out as much as you can about the priorities and directions of the company, as well as the interests, tastes, preferences, likes and dislikes of the individual to whom you are speaking, you can't afford the time to ask long, information-freighted questions. Even if they worked – and they never do.

You should start with short, open questions, move to clarifiers/probing questions and end with closed questions.

The definition of an open question is that it can't be answered with an affirmative or negative.

Questions beginning 'How,' 'Where,' and 'Which' tend, by their nature, to be open.

Questions beginning 'When' or 'Do you...' tend to be closed. So a question like, 'How did you get the company from a tiny start-up to a global trader in such a short time?' allows the person you're interrogating to present you with a big, broad exposition about their company, whereas, 'Do you think entrepreneurship is inherited?' may get you a, 'Yes,' or a 'No' with a full stop attached.

At the beginning, you don't have to worry about the quality of the information you're eliciting or whether it matches the list of essentials to be covered that you wrote at the back of your clipboard. That's for later. In the early stages of the exercise, you simply want the person to talk freely. A conversation creates a relationship. A questionnaire never does.

My mother worked as a market researcher for many years and was struck by how obedient her respondents were. She administered a questionnaire to them and they responded monosyllabically. She maintained that the only time she got interesting new information out of people was when she hit the big empty space in the questionnaire designed to capture the answer to the question, 'Is there anything you'd like to add?'

When you meet a prospective client, you want to get them talking and you want them to get a sense of the level of attention you're paying to them. I'll come to listening skills later in this chapter. The kind of questioning that is needed here should help your respondent to delve more deeply into what they're telling you. This kind of questioning moves the discussion from the general to the specific, from the conceptual to the exemplified, as in the following examples:

- Give me an example of…?
- What exactly would you see as…?
- Why is that so significant?
- To what extent will that affect…?
- How precisely will that work?
- You talk of x. What's the immediate implication of this?
- Expand on that for me.

Clarifiers should always use positive, not negative phrasing. Never begin a clarifier with 'But…' Every time that word is used, it creates a cognitive loop of negativity. Learn to replace, 'But,' with, 'And…' Use clarifiers like:

- Interesting. Explain to me how…
- What you've just said is clearly significant in your thinking. Why is it so significant?

Your asking to have things that come up clarified gets the other person to work. It is the opportunity for you to get the evidence to back any assertion the CEO, CFO or department head may voice to you. It also affords you the opportunity to employ the hypothetical:

- If that scenario were to play out, what would you do?
- What advantages do you foresee for the different options?

It's inevitable, particularly when you're new to this stage of strategic selling, that you'll want to respond to what the other person is saying. Let's say they mention that their current accounting package doesn't allow them to access their gross profit on a daily basis. If your alternative package can show them their gross profit at the end of every business day, the temptation is to say so and to begin to talk about the difference the package has made to other clients. Don't. Bite your tongue. Here's the rule: anything you say in this encounter that doesn't have a question mark after it is questionable. How's that for a paradox?

What it means is that you should be asking, asking, asking. Not telling. Even when an opportunity is provided to you which is so perfect, you're convinced it will never happen again and that if you fail to capitalise on it, right now, you will be struck by a thunderbolt, control yourself and keep asking questions. Including stupid questions. Don't pretend to understand more than you actually do, because it will vitiate the value of some of what you capture, making it less useful in the final proposal. Just say, straight up, that you don't fully understand that point and ask for it to be explained again.

Make sure, as you ask your questions, to use the name of the company and not to yellow-pack it by referring to 'companies like yours.' The individual in front of you is not interested in companies like the one they own or run, only in their own specific company.

You may, at least in the beginning, find yourself worrying, while the other person is talking, that you won't have a good question to ask when they finish. Close down the worry, because it will get in the way of your hearing what they're saying. Remember too that they're not interested in your questions. Be consoled by the knowledge that if they come to the end of a point and you can't figure out where to go next, a number of options are at your disposal. One of them is silence – the silence that says, 'You're fascinating. Say more.' Most respondents, in this situation, will fill a silence that lasts more than three seconds.

Another way to solve the missing question problem is simply to repeat their last words: 'Equitable, open and ethical?' This will encourage them to expand on one or all of the concepts listed.

Alternatively, you can say, 'This is fascinating. Expand on the last point, please.'

Towards the end of the interview is the time for closed questions, the ones which allow only a yes/no answer, for example:

- Is your preference for X or Y?
- Given the possibility of A or B, which would be your preferred approach?

Closed questions must be simple. They should never be double-headed, as a double-headed or multiple-choice question creates confusion. This is an example of a poor closed question as it does not offer a clear-cut choice between two alternatives, A and Z, instead muddying the water by including Y:

- Which do you think would be the better approach, A or Z and do you think it would be important to take Y into consideration?

Towards the end of an encounter is also the time to make connections between elements of what you have heard:

- You talked earlier about leverage – how does that relate to this point?

Whenever you can, move beyond eliciting data and look for the viewpoint on or personal attitude to the data being provided:

- This must have been a difficult choice for you personally?
- How did you react when this situation arose?

As you come near the end of the meeting, the nature of your questioning should indicate this. This is the point at which you double-check the information you've received thus far and get the respondent to prioritise and make choices:

- As I understand what you're saying, your short-term imperative is to claw back market share but that this doesn't rule out acquisitions, as long as they follow the direction you've set?
- So it's not just a matter of ensuring downsizing in the manufacturing plant. You're also committed to redeploying people in the least disruptive way you can manage?

This is the only time in the discussion that you're allowed to display knowledge. Except that it must be knowledge gained in the earlier part of the interview:

Hang on a second. You've told me that you have real problems achieving buy-in to new quality standards and that you're not happy with the division between administration and manufacturing. As far as you are concerned, which of these is the more urgent problem to solve?

If you've done the rest of the interview properly, at this point the person you're questioning should have forgotten that you are questioning them and moved on to a situation where they're simply thinking aloud in your presence. A considerable body of research suggests that people's opinions and the direction of their thinking are often moulded by the questions they're asked. You'll know that this is happening – and that the executive you're meeting feels they're gaining something from it – if they say, at some point, 'D'you know, I don't think I've ever talked about this to anybody else up to now,' or, 'I've never said this to anybody else until today.' Those comments underscore the level of trust you have generated, rather than validating the cleverness of your questioning.

LISTENING: YOUR UNDIVIDED ATTENTION

Always remember that the single most effective relationship-building skill is listening: giving another human being your undivided attention. Astute questioning is a great asset to a salesperson: acute listening is an essential. And the listening needs to be a country mile away from the sharp attention that might be given by a detective superintendant to a suspect or by a senior counsel to a witness. The listening we have in mind is simply interest on steroids.

The father of psychology, William James, noted that the fundamental human need is to be appreciated. That's what active, productive listening delivers. Because it registers the importance of the person you are meeting and underlines your comprehension of their priorities and demands, it is the pivotal dealmaker skill. Research indicates that the less you talk and the more you listen, the more impact you have and the more other people find you interesting and wise.

We are not good at listening, in Ireland. If we're honest with ourselves, we'll admit that we're listening to our own upcoming answer half the time rather than fully attending to what's actually being said. What we're doing, when that happens, is wilfully turning off both a vital source of information and a connection to a good relationship. Small wonder, then, that one of the recurring complaints in breakups, whether these breakups be marital or business, is, 'He/she/the boss/my partner never listens to me.' When my company does communications audits for companies, the failure of management to listen is one of the constant criticisms made by staff at all levels. Learning to listen, really listen, is the best favour you can do for yourself, your friendships, your romantic life and your career.

Learning to listen means, first of all, paying attention to the terms and habits of speech, including metaphors and analogies, that are the cognitive fingerprint of the other person. Men, as a gender, are much more likely than women to use analogies from war or sport. But that's a crude differentiator. If you pay attention to and make note of the way another person uses language, you could write a reasonably authoritative psychological profile of them, because their language will reveal their sources of reference, the books they read and the people who had an impact on their thinking and whether they are optimistic or pessimistic, assertive or passive. In addition, quoting people back to themselves, using the words they actually used, develops a relationship.

I have already mentioned the fact that most of us tend to listen for what's familiar, what we've encountered earlier. That's where we're comfortable. But when you're interviewing a prospective client, you need to listen for differences, for what's new to you. This will allow you to individuate the client or client company.

One of the reasons you should not be dependent on a questionnaire is that constantly referring to bits of paper gets in the way of your watching how the person you are speaking to behaves. By listening with your eyes, you will spot the issues he/she regards as routine and the ones they see as significant. You will identify the areas (and sometimes the people) that bother them and the ones that they're confident and comfortable with. In addition, if you're maintaining reasonable eye contact with them, you may not have to voice questions: a raised eyebrow or a nod will keep them talking.

And while we're on the subject of keeping them talking, be wary of what are euphemistically called 'vocal affirmations'. These are the little moans and grunts and phrases of agreement that slide out of us in every situation. Keep them to a minimum.

It's always useful, just as you're folding up your papers, to say, 'By the way, is there any question I really should have asked you? Anything I should know about before you throw me out?' People frequently offer amazingly helpful added value in response to questions like these.

When you're done with your questions and your listening, tell the person in specific terms how valuable their input was and skedaddle out of there as quickly as you can. Sit in the car in the car park and make notes of any observations your recording device won't have captured and transcribe the recording as quickly as possible after the interview, because your memory of impressions surrounding what was actually said will be freshest at this point.

Then you'll be ready to write your proposal.

6

WRITING THE PROPOSAL

Your written proposal or response to tender (which is dealt with in more detail in Chapter 7) is the fourth stage of the five-stage process of strategic selling.

'It's the definition of a service, that sales can work only when the marketing is correct. There has to be a basic logic that this thing can work for the customer, and secondly in what fashion is it going to work, so you have to have done your thinking.' This is the view of Jerry Kennelly, the man who sold his Stockbyte business to Getty Images for more than €110 million and went on to start several other businesses while devoting a goodly chunk of his time to fostering young entrepreneurs through the Endeavour programme. One of the points he hammers home to these entrepreneurs is that a business won't grow if you think you can look at sales as an add-on at the end of all other processes. He maintains:

> The fundamental of any business I've ever been involved in is that it's something that's going to make life better for the customer. Is it something that is going to save them time, money? Is it

going to be lots better than the previous product line? Ideally it is going to be productive. So when you're creating anything it's got to be created for the customer.

He's right, especially when it comes to the kind of products and services that fall under the heading of 'strategic purchases'. Your proposal or response to tender is your opportunity to demonstrate a number of key strengths:

1. That you understand precisely what the company needs, not just what it wants
2. That you understand the business into which your offering must fit and which your product or service must enable or enhance
3. That you grasp the operational changes required by the introduction of your product or service and can facilitate the streamlined installation or implementation of this product or service
4. That you've already supplied similar products or services in comparable organisations
5. That you're qualified and accredited, in areas where this is relevant
6. That you can supply the product or service in a cost-effective way.

Not all these elements these apply to every strategic sale, but most of them do, so let's address them in more detail.

WHAT YOU MUST SHOW IN YOUR PROPOSAL OR RESPONSE TO TENDER

1. That you understand precisely what the company needs, not just what it wants

At one point, one of our trainers, commissioned to improve the skills of salespeople attached to a computer firm, cancelled the training after the first day, when he discovered, as he put it, that, 'These people are selling technology they don't understand to people who don't know what they really need.' Because the sales team had only a smattering of computer knowledge but a lot of enthusiasm, they were managing to sell systems to customers who later realised that the technology didn't do what they needed it to do. The supplier's electronic engineers then had to be directed to the customers' websites to tweak the technology and put in patches to bring it up to spec. The end result was that the supplier was losing a small amount of money on each and every sale. Not good.

If you base your next step on the transcript of your interview with the executive from the company, you can avoid this kind of selling. You can, instead, demonstrate that you understand what the company wants as well as what it needs. Wherever possible in your proposal, use the words of the executive, either within quotation marks or in your own text, when describing these needs. That way, you establish, not just that you paid attention when he or she gave you their valuable time, but that you captured and understood what you were offered. It also means you're literally speaking their language.

2. That you understand the business into which your offering must fit, and which your product or service must enable or enhance

In the early days of sales training, much emphasis was placed on discussing benefits, as opposed to features. In other words, good salespeople realised that explaining the innards of a car or computer to a potential customer was a complete waste of time. They moved, instead, to describing what those features enabled the item they were selling to do. The benefit lay in the performance of the feature.

Now, selling has moved a step further. Now it is essential to show that you understand the kind of business your potential customer has, so that the benefits you outline make immediate, applicable sense to them: 'Oh, yes, if I was doing X, this application would save me ten minutes on every task. Wow.'

Your proposal must individuate the client company and must show that you find it interesting and different and that you understand that these differences will inform their purchase of a service or product.

3. That you grasp the operational changes required by the introduction of your product or service and can facilitate the streamlined installation or implementation of this product or service

The nature of a strategic purchase is that it tends to demand retraining of the people who use it – or at least some change in the way they do things. Change may be required for the user's safety, to bring them up to speed with a new application or to help them to understand the wider possibilities presented by the purchase of a product or a service. Delivering a truckload of neatly boxed technology doesn't solve a customer's problem. What solves a customer's problems is delivering technology and leaving only when it's up and working and the staff fully understands how to use it and what it can produce.

4. That you've already supplied similar products or services to comparable organisations

It's not enough to have a great machine or a great training programme at a great price. You must remove your customer's anxieties and this is best done by explaining how what you are proposing has worked elsewhere. Even better if you can direct the customer to telephone someone at the site to which you've supplied the product or service, having first primed this person to ensure he or she will say helpful relevant positive things about you and your offering. Before you mention a company in a tender or proposal, ensure that they have no confidentiality requirements. If you're not sure, phone and ask them. It will remind them of you and might spark them into ordering something new from you or your company.

5. That you're qualified and accredited, in areas where this is relevant

Some companies buy exclusively from suppliers with a particular accreditation: others don't have this requirement. You'll have found this out in your interview on their premises. Respond appropriately.

6. That you can supply the products or services cost-effectively
Many tenders require service-suppliers to break out the hours to be worked by differing levels of executives within their company. It's endlessly tedious and most of us would prefer to say, 'Just give us 25K and we'll all be happy.' But when in Rome… Be very careful about your costing. Don't go in so low that it will cripple your organisation and make sure that you can sustain the price you quote (in the case of a service) over the entire course of the contract.

7

RESPONDING TO TENDER

One of the most successful writers of tenders in Ireland is Dermot McCrum of Strand Communications. Dermot's a strategic consultant and has laid down these top ten tips for tender-writing:

1. Assign a bid director and bid manager if the tender is large enough to warrant it. The bid director is responsible for everything and ultimately he or she decides what goes in and what stays out. The bid manager is the person who pulls all the material together from various people, under the direction of the bid director. He or she is authorised to persuade/cajole/threaten with immediate extinction anyone who has to deliver material within deadline.

2. Read the document carefully. Twice. Three times. Order the requirements into segments of work around topics or around people who will write the response for you.

3. Respond to what you are asked for in the

tender. Ask questions to clarify elements for your own understanding but be aware that your questions and answers will be distributed to anyone else who is tendering. But if there is lack of clarity don't be afraid to ask.

4. Canvassing will disqualify. It does – exactly what it says on the tin. This doesn't stop you researching other aspects of the market, finding out useful information that will provide insight and evidence for the proposal you're making.

5. Give yourself sufficient time. Tender documents take time to write – properly. Trying to write a tender forty-eight hours before the deadline will drive you and your staff berserk and the pressure will be evident in the presentation.

6. If you have the budget and time, consider getting some research done or an independent authority to verify or support any specific claims you make about your company, your services, or elements/ approaches of the proposal you're submitting.

7. It doesn't have to be *The Book of Kells*, but getting a properly laid-out, typeset, printed bid document can help to support your corporate pride in the products or services you supply A ten-page, hastily assembled, plastic binder folder might present the

wrong image or be a distraction to the assessors.

8. Examine carefully the assessment criteria and the marks for each criterion, and concentrate your time, energy and depth of response accordingly: if, for instance, background and experience get 10 per cent, and the quality of the proposal and its cost get thirty per cent each, you should know where to focus most attention.

9. Find a proofreader – a really good one. Nothing grates more than a nicely prepared document that has, on its first page, two spelling errors, three wrong names and poor grammar or syntax.

10. The deadline is the deadline is the deadline. Excuses – the dog ate your homework, the courier stopped for a pizza, a pipe burst and drowned your photocopier – won't get your proposal inside the door if it's delivered late. Leave enough time and set false deadlines if necessary. If the tender has to be in by 12pm on Tuesday, have it finished and delivered by 4pm on Monday.

Bear in mind how much all this may cost the company. Make sure to debrief after each proposal or tender, to quantify if it was worth your while. Be ruthlessly honest: stop tendering if you're not winning a high enough proportion of contracts.

A client company of the Communications Clinic, after a day's facilitation by one of our senior consultants, made radical changes in its marketing strategy and tactics, not because we'd suggested them – we hadn't – but because, once they'd had the chance to stand back and look at what they were doing, they were able to see clearly how little of it actually fed into eventual sales. As the session concluded, their CFO summarised what they'd learned and decided, 'We're going to stop shelling out a fortune to pursue every E-Tender that comes up. Our hit rate, compared to our effort, has been poor. Instead, we're going to concentrate, this coming year, on growing existing companies and getting referral business.'

It was a good decision for this company. E-Tenders are a little like emails and text messages; they carry an unreal urgency with them. Many companies trawl the emerging tender list every week. Some do it every day. They respond to any tender in their area, sometimes expending an enormous amount of time and creativity on research, writing, design and presentation. That's bad enough. Worse is when a company congratulates itself on its *failure* to get a contract, using feedback from the process to reassure itself that the selection process was a close-run thing. Being a close-run second doesn't justify self-congratulation. Either you won or you lost and if you lost, you should have an acute understanding of what the loss cost you, financially and in terms of time.

One of the crucial losses implicit in constant, reflexive response to requests for tender is the loss of time. Executives of the company mentioned earlier worked out that the company was spending, on average, ninety-six working hours per tender. 'But they usually take no more than a couple of days,' one of the managers said.

It was when they investigated this that they realised that 'a couple of days' usually meant three full days, if you counted the frenetic last minute all-nighters they regularly pulled. Anton, our facilitator, then pushed the managers to work out which of them tended to do the most work on any tender. The owner/CEO, was the response.

'What's his charge-out rate?' Anton asked. 'In other words, if you're selling his time to a client, what do you charge the client per hour?'

€500, came the answer.

The owner himself did the math: 'Fifty hours at that rate adds up to €25,000. So every tender is costing us, between my time and everybody else's time, as well as printing, design and so on, almost €50,000 a throw. The yearly retainer fee on the typical contract we'd win that way is around €60,000. So we're spending fifty to get ten.'

'If we had a more streamlined way of doing it, we could bring down the cost,' their accountant pointed out.

'The issue isn't whether we could do it better,' the owner replied. 'The issue is whether we should be doing it at all. You and I get business all the time just by meeting people and talking to them. Why don't we just concentrate on what we're good at and stop putting ourselves under pointless pressure?'

8

CLOSING THE SALE

I hope you'll be puzzled as you read this chapter. Puzzled about the title. Because the chapter is about the kind of presentation you may have to make to a prospective client, rather than about killer phrases you hope will cause the client to roll over and want their tummy tickled.

The verbal discussion of what you're offering is the fifth stage in the five-stage selling process. The fourth – the written proposal – has established that you understand what a potential customer wants and needs. In the case of a request for tender coming from a government department or state organisation, this written submission will have either disqualified you from further contention (because you have failed to fill in one of the sections, clearly aren't qualified to provide the service they want or have priced it so expensively that they couldn't afford it) or qualified you to meet the prospective client for a final examination of the detail.

In the PR business, companies who are rivals, red in tooth and claw, nonetheless share information at this point:

'You been called to present?'

'Yeah – and so have Tweetie Pie and the Grinch.'

'That all?'

'Seems so.'

'Thanks be to J.'

Finding out who else has been called to present tells you a lot about the prospective client. In the case of the conversation above, both PR competitors would, on the basis of the selection of four companies to present, be clear that:

- The clients wanted a solidly established agency, rather than a start-up.
- The clients wanted a company with a specific skillset.
- The clients were fast decision-makers.
- Money was not the clients' key consideration

After that, the interests of the two competitors would diverge and they wouldn't talk again until the process was over.

Preparing for the fifth stage of the five-stage strategic selling process follows the same rules as the rest of the process. It starts with research, with finding out information that will help the supplier to deliver the kind of presentation the client prefers.

Some of this information will have been found out during the interview with their executive. It makes sense, for example, to ask the executive:

- How many people from his company will be at the presentation and their names, titles, function and priorities

- Whether the company likes PowerPoint presentations or not
- Whether it would be appropriate to leave extra documentation or not
- How long they like suppliers to speak for
- How long the question and answer section of the negotiation will be
- Location
- Time
- Available technology
- Parking provision

You will then craft your presentation to meet each of these preferences while selecting from and prioritising what is in your proposal. You should never set out simply to repeat, when on your feet in front of your prospective client, everything you've said in print in your written proposal or response to tender. You're there to be:

- Interesting
- Understandable
- Memorable

You're there to further the relationship you have already established with these potential clients. This means you must look at them and talk to them as if they were human beings. You're there to add value to what you've already given them in print.

REHEARSAL TIME

When you have roughed out the key issues you want your audience to hear and remember, it's time to reality-test your presentation. Having a word with your champion within the company may be a good idea. Remember that you (and possibly others) have met the executive in charge of this contract and, by asking questions, may have caused them to widen or shift their thoughts about what they need. Your champion may be aware of such changes and will be in a position to help you tilt your presentation to cover them.

When you're fairly happy with the general content, it's time to rehearse. If it's an important enough contract, you may want to get professional help. In any week, staff at the Communications Clinic sits through presentations on everything from financial audits to new waste-handling machinery. We then ask the obvious – and the difficult – questions. Even if the contract is not of sufficient scale to justify getting professional help, get a number of colleagues or friends around you and make the presentation to them. Let them ask questions. Answer the questions. Then, if you can, take a ten-minute break before the debrief. The reason for the ten-minute break is this. Even in that short a period of time, the short-term memory of the people who sat through your speech will have begun to shed items from what you said. Believe it or not, this is helpful, because it quickly shows you what, within the presentation, you managed to make especially memorable and what requires more work, whether this takes the form of repetition or of a better means of illustrating it.

Because this dry run may happen only a day or two before the real pitch, be wary of allowing your colleagues to come up with advice that will serve only to discomfit and unnerve you. Tell them what you want to know and bar them from telling you what you don't want to know. You don't, for example, want to know what they would say in your situation. You're the one who will be trying to close the sale, not them, and you are unlikely to do a confident job unless you're using your own material and frames of reference that are familiar to you.

Something borrowed may be great at a wedding but it can stick out uncomfortably in a business pitch. And as for something blue – forget it. You're not there to entertain. You're there to inform.

Here's where I need to knock on the head – yet again – a stereotype that never goes away: the concept of the salesperson as a fast-talking phoney. When you're making a presentation to a company in order to persuade them to buy a product or service from you that will make a sizeable dent in their yearly budget, fast-talking and phoney won't cut it. Authenticity tends to work.

Being authentic in a presentation means using real words rather than words with evening dresses and top hats on them. It means talking to other human beings rather than to An Audience. It means watching the individual or group you're talking to, so you notice when you're hammering a point too hard or confusing them with figures. It means transporting the best of yourself into this pressured situation, so, by the time you're finished, the Them and Us configuration has diminished and those present have become collaborators around the solution to a problem or the building of a success. So in your rehearsal, don't set out to impress and do ask your friends to alert you to anything you're saying that doesn't sound comfortable coming out of your mouth.

Above all, while preparing, don't allow the presentation to take on the shape of a major theatrical performance. What you need to demonstrate, when you get in front of the client-to-be, is what the psychologist Robert Sternberg (in *Successful Intelligence: How Practical and Creative Intelligence Determine Success in Life*) calls 'practical intelligence': things like 'knowing what to say to whom, knowing when to say it and knowing how to say it for maximum effect.' It is procedural: it is about knowing how to do something without necessarily knowing why you know it or being able to explain it. It's practical in nature: that is, it's not knowledge for its own sake. It's knowledge that helps you to read situations correctly and get what you want. And, critically it's a kind of intelligence distinct from the sort of analytical ability measured by IQ. To use the technical term, general intelligence and practical intelligence are 'orthogonal' (at right angles to each other): the presence of one doesn't imply the presence of the other. You can have lots of analytical intelligence and very little practical intelligence or lots of practical intelligence and not much analytical intelligence, or – if you're very lucky – you can have lots of both.

Practical intelligence gets damped down when people try to imitate other people's style or method of pitching. Just concentrate on establishing yourself in the pitch situation as a reliable, trustworthy partner or potential partner, with the client's best interests in mind. Remember, if you genuinely believe you have something they need, you don't need to get into false performance mode.

The knowledge that you understand them, their business and the relevance of your offering to them should inform your approach to preparing for their questions. This is not a game for them and they should not suddenly become enemies in your eyes when they ask tough questions. They ask the questions you'd ask if you were in their shoes – which is why you need to put yourself in their shoes in advance of the real thing. Write down every question you believe they're likely to ask. Now, write down the questions you hope they'll never ask.

You may, for example, hope that they won't ask you what flexibility you have around price. But what if they do? Go back to the personality profile you built up of their executive. Are they the kind of person who will want to show off to their colleagues that they can screw every last penny out of you? If they are, you'd better price your offering so that you can retreat just a little from that price without going broke. If, however, the client is one of those logical people who wants to come to grips with the constituent elements of the overall cost, you can decide in advance that the cost is non-negotiable but you will have to explain every bit of it in the presentation and defend it in the question and answer session.

Rehearsing the presentation and any potential questions may kick up new issues not covered in your proposal. If it improves or changes what you are going to be offering, it may be worth ringing either your champion or the person you interviewed, to give them a heads-up that you're planning to introduce an issue outside the proposal because you think it would be valuable. (If it changes cost or personnel or time allocated, you can't do this in a tender. Any deviation from the spec tends to panic people operating a tender.) It's also acceptable to ring and check a detail that may have become unclear as you probed it.

(Again, in a tender process, remember that if you go back with even the simplest question, the organisers will solemnly input the answer and send it to all other tenderers. In some cases, this is no skin off your nose and the answer mystifies those who don't know the rationale behind your question. In other cases, having your question revealed by this broad-spectrum distribution is grossly unfair, because it provides an insight or angle to your competitors they might never have reached unaided. This is one of those examples of fairness, as dreamed up by a barking bureaucrat, which, to any sane person, is so obviously *un*fair as not to merit discussion. Live with it. You have no choice.)

PRESENTATION AS A PART OF SELLING

One of the best presentations we ever heard of was one a prospective architect of an extension to a golf clubhouse made to the members, pitching for the funding. It was a major piece of work and was going to be very expensive so he knew he had to make a good case.

He hired a cherry-picker, taking photographs aloft from all sides of the clubhouse. On the night of the presentation he had the results blown up and attached to the walls around the meeting room, covering the windows. He stood up, said, 'Gentlemen, the view from the first floor…' and sat down again. He got his funding.

Now that is good use of visual aids – not a PowerPoint in sight. The lesson we need to learn from his success was that he was able to move his audience from a position of worry or concern to having them envisage, on a concrete basis, a desired future state. That's what a selling presentation needs to do. Sure, members of the club had questions but the backdrop was the future: it was exciting and focused not just on their needs, but on their wants.

Like any good presenter, the architect in question started with his audience: who they were, their interests, their anxieties and their concerns. He thought of his communication task – to convince them to part with large wads of cash for quite a radical approach to extending their clubhouse. He built his presentation on their strong desire for more space, emphasising the benefits and advantages of his preferred option. Crucially, he handled questions of cost *after* he'd got his audience to imagine the future. Once he'd managed to get them to imagine the future, the members would find it difficult to abandon that future, even if it was going to cost them a bit more than they'd bargained for.

I'm not saying you should inflate your price and sell hard to achieve it but that you should ask yourself what your buying decision-maker wants for themselves and the company. Get to know them, their role and the way they measure their own and the company's success. Then, and only then, begin to work out how you can help them to imagine their winning future. Because this is about them, not you. Or, more accurately, it's about their win – then yours.

As we saw in Chapter 5, you need not only to know lots about the executive you meet and their company, you need to be able to think yourself into their shoes. One of the Dublin-based radio stations has a question in large format on every wall in the office: what would Orla say? Orla is their target listener. When new staff members are appointed, management tell them about Orla: she's thirty-two, married, no kids, two dogs, a four-wheel drive and a job as a fashion buyer. They have personified her: in other words they know her age, her likes and dislikes and where she lives.

For radio broadcasting, it is really important to personify one's audience. Everyone listens as an individual. When you are making a sales presentation to a group (and you usually are), each member of your audience is also listening as an individual. Find out as much as you possibly can about each individual. Whether your notional individual, your Orla, is a man or a woman, put yourself in their shoes, and imagine what they see as success. Then work out how you, with your product or service, can help them to achieve this success.

Don't exclude the rest of the group to concentrate on the person you perceive to be the decision-maker. If you do this blatantly and exclusively you will get everyone else's backs up. Focus on other individuals as you highlight benefits and emotional wins in their specific areas. For example, the user influencer (the person on the panel who will interface most closely with your product or service every day: the person who has to get everyone to operate the new machine) should hear about the new machine's capacity to save at least an hour a day per operator. This information should be addressed specifically to him.

Be specific. Paint the tangible picture of the future for the people who are listening to you. Show them how they can achieve this situation and when, with examples of similar deals you've engineered with others. You must do this early in the presentation. Don't forget the *primacy*, recency, relevance rule. This is the rule, derived from social and cognitive psychology, that indicates the importance of first impressions. In short, research indicates the people are inclined to remember (in this order): 1) what they heard or noticed first; 2) the last thing they heard (it is this that leads to comments like, 'I'm easily influenced – I always agree with the last person to speak'); and 3) what affects themselves (we find topics that are irrelevant to our lives or interests difficult to engage with). So begin by making an impact. Catch their attention, as the architect did with the golf-club members.

Speak simply and vividly. My advice is that you shouldn't use PowerPoint if possible and this is something I expand on later in this chapter.

Remind your listeners that everything you've done for their organisation so far has worked out well. Point to your reliability – remind them how you stuck with the staff member who struggled with one of your products until he got the hang of it and how much you enjoyed doing it.

If you've never worked with the company before, making reference to deals with others – the more prestigious the clients the better – will be a reassurance as evidence supporting your claims. Having senior people in these companies willing to talk directly with the key decision-maker will be a valuable plank in your selling platform. (In time to come, the new people will do the same for you – if you over-deliver on their expectations.)

Later the people to whom you are presenting will

compare notes. At this point, you want the key decision-maker to be your champion. You want them to be so convinced of your value to them and to the organisation that they'll fight your battles for you. You need as many champions as you can get.

All of what I've said up to now in this chapter is about reinforcing yourself in the pitch situation as a reliable, trustworthy partner or potential partner, with the client's best interests in mind. You should, of course, have done this at every stage of your work with this company and individual – but sometimes people need to be reminded of salient facts. It will be particularly salient if your competitors are presenting too.

Your next step is to let them know you understand their current challenges and goals. If you've done your homework, this part is easy, because you do understand them. Make sure your understanding is up to date. If an item on today's news is relevant, include its implications for their industry and business. This way, you're not just feeding back to them what they said to you two weeks ago. Parrot quotes won't develop your relationship.

Your understanding of their challenges and goals should lead seamlessly into how you can help them to meet them. And that's what you're offering – your tailored, targeted help. While you are doing this you need to keep observing them, checking for any fall-off in understanding or support. If they are also meeting competitors, they'll probably maintain a professional (meaning objective) demeanour – 'to give everyone a fair crack of the whip', they might say. If you've developed a robust understanding of the key decision-maker and their company, you'll be able to take that for what it is, while still gauging your impact accurately.

Now do you see why we said, 'Don't use PowerPoint'? If you're still inclined to use PowerPoint, let me ask you this question: how well will you be able to speak simply, vividly and with impact while observing your listeners closely for nuances in their reactions and comments, maintaining and developing the relationship and responding to their cues, while managing a laptop and projector? How well will they be able to connect with you when you distract them with slide after slide?

POWERPOINT OR NOT?

I know that, to many people, 'presentation' equals Power-Point. This is simply wrong. PowerPoint is, by definition, a visual aid and in the scale of effectiveness of visual aids, it's down round number three or four. The very best visual aid is a sample – but only if it's easily understood and operated. For example if you want to explain the features of a camera, giving one to your target and taking them through what it can do for them is helpful. If your product is small, fidgety and difficult to operate, enlarged pictures and explanatory diagrams might work better.

Photographs, models and maps are good visual aids – remember our architect. Remember that he was selling a *concept*, not a product. When the photographic display had been absorbed, the rest of the presentation was his pitch, where he used his mastery of his profession and his understanding of the members' needs and wants to convince them to go for his solution. He was able to use his voice, his face, his body to make the concept concrete.

They were not being distracted from what he had to say by a new PowerPoint slide every minute. He had their undivided attention, so he was able to gauge reactions, anticipate objections and manage expectations.

When we ask participants on presentation courses at the Communications Clinic to describe really good presentations they've attended, they remark on qualities in the presenter: 'She was engaging', they say, or, 'He talked directly to us'. When we drill down into details of the presenter's behaviour they say eye contact is very important. How well can you maintain eye contact with people when you have slides to manage and – worse again – to read from?

The current use of PowerPoint has two major flaws. Firstly, people forget it's a visual aid and give us loads of text to read. If you give an audience something to read, they'll do just that and they'll be down at the bottom of the slide while you're still on Bullet 1. Now you've really lost contact with them. (By the way, if you give handouts in advance, you will achieve the same disconnect or an even worse one: your audience will obediently read what you give them to read and will be on Page 12 before you're finished Page 2. Most of us read faster than we speak.)

The second major fault with how people use PowerPoint is data overload. You have a presentation to put together, and, in mortal fear and 'survivor' mode, you decide to give them every tiniest bit of information you have on the topic, instead of starting with what the audience needs. Your audience can't possibly take all this in, especially as you've disregarded their interests and concerns – you haven't given them a reason to care. The obvious outcome is what Professor Harold R. Tufte (in *The Cognitive Style of PowerPoint*) calls 'Death by PowerPoint':

> The popular PowerPoint templates (ready-made designs) usually weaken verbal and spatial reasoning, and almost always corrupt statistical analysis...At a minimum, a presentation format should do no harm. Yet the PowerPoint style routinely disrupts, dominates and trivializes content. Thus PowerPoint presentations too often resemble a school play – very loud, very slow and very simple.
>
> The practical conclusions are clear. PowerPoint is a competent slide manager and projector. But rather than supplementing a presentation, it has become a substitute for it. Such misuse ignores the most important rule of speaking: Respect your audience.

'But...' the younger and more recently graduated of you will be protesting, 'I won't look prepared if I don't use PowerPoint. They'll think I'm not professional.' Or even, 'Everyone else will be using slides.' When I was a teenager and my mother vetoed the latest disco, I countered with, 'Everyone else will be going.' Her withering response, like that of all mothers down the ages, was, 'If they all ran out under a bus, would you do the same?' If people who attend presentations tell us that slides, especially text slides, mostly don't work, why would we continue to use them?

In the final pitch situation we're concerned with here, using PowerPoint would be a pointless intrusion into an established relationship. Instead of casting you in the light of a professional, it could make you seem like a total amateur, someone who didn't trust themselves enough to develop the existing relationship further and build on the rapport painstakingly constructed over a long period. Don't do it. Work *with* your negotiation partners, not against them.

What you should aim to do at a presentation is to leave pictures in the heads of the people to whom you present. Descriptions can do that. Storylines can do it. By 'storylines' I mean a chronological explanation of an installation so that everybody present can almost see it happening in front of them as you talk. If you explain something in visual detail, you force people to concentrate in order to 'get' what you're talking about, whereas, if you use PowerPoint, the disadvantage is that those present don't feel the need to concentrate quite as hard.

QUESTIONS AND ANSWERS

Remember that the question-and-answer session is another opportunity for you to cover, using different illustrations, points you particularly want the client to understand and remember. It may also be an opportunity to close the sale, after you've gone through the four stages of the process. Obviously, this doesn't apply in a tender situation where you're up against a number of other contenders and where it would be inappropriate to ask for the sale.

If your champion is at the presentation, beware of favouring them in your answers, The champion will be of most use to you if they don't get labelled as your best pal. Get into the habit, in rehearsal, of taking even negative questions positively. Some questioners naturally cast negative phraseology around each query, so it arrives sounding halfway between a complaint and an attack. Remember that your interests and theirs are parallel, not in opposition, so whatever they ask you is a useful way to test the strength of your case. Welcome the question. Do not narrow your eyes at the questioner or give them a brief cold answer before turning your gaze back to the guy who's lobbing you much softer balls.

Closing the sale is one of those areas about which more bullshit has been written (and included in training programmes) than any other. Most of them are predicated on an understanding of closing the sale as the concluding act in a con job so they take the form of trick questions or of coercive concluding questions that require the client to provide the seller with a delivery date.

This extremely dated approach to selling is the basis of David Mamet's terrifying play (and film) *Glengarry Glenross*, which portrays successful salesmen as driven psychopaths who regard all prospects as sub-human moronic potential enemies. This kind of selling assumes that a series of manipulative models and metrics and approaches applied to human beings invariably pop out a sale. If slavishly followed, they allow for the sale of sand to Arabs, snow to Inuit and old rope to any passing stranger. This interpretation of selling is what has brought it into disrepute and keeps it there. It degrades those on both sides of what should be a civilised negotiation between honest equals.

The reality is that if you have gone through the five stages I have outlined – you have identified a genuine need of the potential customer; you have discussed this need with them; you have come to an understanding of their business and the mindset of the key buyer; and you have provided, unless you're nuts or a crook or just plain incompetent, something that meets expressed needs at a reasonable cost – the sale should pretty much zip itself up.

Someone once described sales as 'the crises that occur at the end of marketing.' In fact, if the five-stage process I have described is intelligently deployed, sales should be the inevitability that occur at the end of marketing.

INTELLIGENT SELL RATHER THAN HARD SELL

'I'm more a fan of an intelligent sell than a hard sell,' says successful businessman, Kerryman Jerry Kennelly. According to him, salespeople who are successful have a killer instinct that drives them on to be really productive and really clinical about cutting away at a point where someone is not going to make a decision to buy so that they don't over-invest in a relationship. It's not a game of hope, it's not buying lottery tickets.

Kennelly tells a wonderful story – the true story of how he brought the Stockbyte sale to Getty to a successful conclusion. Getty entered exclusive negotiations with Stockbyte after an original auction where Bill Gates's Corbis had been an underbidder (Kennelly had been a major supplier to Getty) and negotiations were in train when for some reason they stalled. Jerry decided he needed to find a way to break the log-jam.

> I called up Jonathan Klein [Getty CEO] one
> day and I said, 'Jonathan, have you ever

been to Puck Fair in Killorglin?'

He said, 'No.'

I said, 'It's a pagan fair. There's a goat – he's called King Puck – he's hoisted on to a stand on the first day of the fair every August. He presides over the town. There's loads of drinking and craic. And there's a horse fair and there's a cattle fair. There's a tradition at the horse fair and the cattle fair that when you buy an animal, the seller bestows a gift on the buyer. And it's called 'luck money'.

I said, 'I want you to pay close attention to that because it's a gift and gifts are never the subject of a negotiation as you know. I want to bestow some luck money on you to get this deal wrapped up. I'm bestowing $10 million luck money to you.'

He said, 'Thank you very much, Jerry.'

If I'd approached that in a different way, you're talking about driving a 45 bus through the fence and it could have resulted in a renegotiation. That did the trick. He needed to deliver for his board. I needed to get the deal across the line and it was time to take one for the team. In the scale of things, $10 million was neither here nor there.

That's why the hard sell doesn't work for any important sale. It doesn't take account of the human emotions involved. Buyers need to want and need the service or product from you. And if they report to someone else, like a board or a CEO, you have to convince them what a good deal it is and make them feel good too.

Significantly, Jerry Kennelly still does business with Getty.

9

SHOCK, HORROR:
YOU DON'T MAKE THE SALE

Now, it is possible, after all that effort, that you won't make the sale. The news that you have not made the sale is what separates sheep from goats and salespeople from those who might be better in another career. The reaction to losing a sale tends to be vivid. It can involve emotions ranging from rage to contrition to despair. Some salespeople go into a total slump and can hardly speak when they get their 'Dear John' letter or phone call. Some do vertical take-off into enraged conspiracy theories: it was a fix from the start, the incumbent was always going to hang on to the contract and probably bribes everybody on the client's side anyway, they don't know what's good for them and to hell with them, we're well out of it.

A third kind of response goes the opposite way by assuming that the client is straight, rational and has some good reason for rejecting what was proffered and that it now behoves the seller to find out precisely why their product or service didn't match the customer's needs.

We'll come back to the research you need to do when you lose a sale but let's start with the people who slump when they encounter rejection. While a great feeling of let-down is understandable, if the salesperson can't pick themselves up and move beyond it within a day or two, they may simply not have the right kind of personality for selling. That doesn't have to be a back-slapping, life-of-the-party, you-gotta-hava-laff personality. It just means having characteristics like a positive attitude, confidence and faith in yourself. These are so important they formed the basis of a study an eminent psychologist conducted in the US some years ago.

Professor Martin Seligman of the University of Pennsylvania wanted to explore the impact of optimism on career success. He figured that being able to handle defeat or rejection would be useful if not essential in business in general and particularly in selling. Because the ratio of yes to no in the sales situation can be so skewed – in some businesses, for every 'yes' the salesperson achieves they meets nine 'nos' – salespeople have to be self-motivating individuals who can bounce back from negatives and learn the mathematics of their craft. An 80/20 situation – you have to make eighty calls in order to get twenty face-to-face meetings – can be tough for people who take the eighty negative responses personally. If the payoff for face-to-face meetings follows the same pattern, the experience can be so discouraging that simply getting out of bed in the morning to embark on climbing this salesman's Mount Everest can be a challenge.

The results of Professor Seligman's research can be found in his book *Learned Optimism*. He established that roughly three quarters of insurance sales representatives in the company he was researching, MetLife, abandoned the job and went to do something quite different within three years. But he also found that optimism played a part in retention. Salespeople tended to stay on the job if they found that they were pretty successful in their early years. Significantly, Seligman found that the ones who did well in those key early years were more likely to be optimists than pessimists.

He administered tests to find out if the salespeople in one company were optimists or pessimists and discovered two devastating truths: pessimists didn't sell anything like the amount of business that optimists sold and they were twice as likely as optimists to abandon the job within the first two years.

Seligman persuaded the insurance company to let him hire a bunch of potential salespeople, not on their previous success rates nor on their academic qualifications but on their high score when it came to optimism. The distinction between the guys he picked and the guys MetLife would normally pick could not have been more pronounced. In some cases, his recruits had actually failed the normal screening tests administered by MetLife.

The year Seligman started his study, MetLife recruited a new set of salespeople in the normal way. Then Seligman's team (who could have been described as optimistic rejects) and the normal team were trained and sent off on the task of selling insurance. Seligman's group outsold the others by 21 per cent.

Optimists win: pessimists lose? Too easy a judgement to make. When anybody undertakes a study of this nature, they have to be wary of the Hawthorne effect, where the enthusiasm generated by being found interesting – being observed by scientists – makes the people being observed perform much better than they normally would. However, Seligman's approach held up even better the second year, when the optimists outsold the other guys by an astonishing 57 per cent.

The fact that optimists were able to deliver so well on sales seemed to derive from their capacity to view each negative or refusal as no more than a necessary stepping stone to several successes. The pessimists, in sharp contrast, were creased by early refusals and tended to make cosmic judgements against themselves: I'm no good at this; I'm a disaster; I'll never make it as a salesperson; I just don't have it and now I dread the next time I have to telephone someone.

Optimists and pessimists have quite different kinds of inner commentary – the voice that reports to each of us on how we're doing.

Let's say two people fall in the street. The pessimist's inner voice says, 'I'm doomed, I've broken my hips/spine/ arms/teeth. I've destroyed my boots/trousers. Someone will steal my briefcase before I can get my act together. Everybody's looking at me and they think I'm a complete fool. I'm always falling. I'm bloody awkward. I never learn'.

The optimist's inner voice says, 'Blast. That uneven surface is a disgrace. I couldn't have avoided it. But I won't miss it the next time. Anyway someone will help me up and I might get them to take me for a cup of coffee.'

I exaggerate – but not much.

Pessimists are easily triggered towards disappointment, depression and disempowerment. Optimists have the same experiences but don't take them personally, learn from them but don't learn negative expectations. They feel in charge of their own lives, take responsibility for their own happiness and own their own careers.

If you apply these distinctions to MetLife's situation, it might strike you that the pessimists, once they knew (if they knew) that their unqualified, indeed rejected competitors on the other team had so significantly outsold them, would judge themselves negatively and feel powerless going into Year 2, whereas the optimists, knowing how much better they'd done, would go in to the second year feeling even more buoyant about themselves. Which feelings would then have contributed to the widening divide between the performances of the two teams during the second twelve months. It's sad to think about the pessimists on the MetLife Team as they faced into the third year, especially with their numbers reduced by the departure of so many from their original cohort. Having started pessimistically, they must, at that stage, have had survivor guilt, to add to their other problems.

Which brings us to the question: should you go into sales if you're not an optimist? I hate to be simplistic but the answer is probably that you shouldn't. In his book, *The Trusted Advisor*, management consultant David Maister maintains that when he is recruiting consultants, he looks for 'the people with the shining eyes'. When my own company advises HR interviewers on the recruitment process, we warn them against employing people they believe are 'not quite right' for the job but who have potential and could be 'grown into' the job. Kerry businessman Jerry Kennelly puts it more succinctly. In every presentation he makes to business people who want to know the secrets of success, he includes a slide which says, with simple directness: 'Don't hire gobshites.' I do not wish to equate pessimists with gobshites but it is worth suggesting that if you tend to catastrophise, if your internal commentary is and always has been negative, if you retreat in the face of challenge, maybe you should think twice before you go into selling. This career may simply not offer you the best opportunity to express your strengths.

Assuming you have some optimism in you, this optimism needs to be consciously strengthened when you go into the selling business. One of the related strengths you need to develop is good judgement. You need to be able to make a decision, based on data, about the point at which a sale has failed. You need to close down your personal sense of failure and move on, without mourning the loss deeply and for a long time. Five years from now, you probably won't even remember the company involved.

Keeping Martin Seligman's study in mind, you need to manage your attitude so that it is always one of optimistic enquiry, because you will make no progress whatever if you decide, 'That's just me, I'm no good at selling.' You will need to unlearn this pessimistic response. If you don't, you're saying to yourself, 'I can't change: my life is never going to be any better than it is now.' Instead, learn to build a dismissal box into which you can close off failures, having decided, 'Well, that was a disaster. But it was a once-off. The next call will be mighty.'

After a rejection, whether it happens after the first phone call or the last presentation, one of the dangers is the temptation to over-analyse what has happened, creating a range of conspiracy theories to explain it away.

This speculation adds up to a kind of static in your head, stopping you from thinking. Cut out the random noise and concentrate on the information. It's impossible to be rejected without some information passing hands, even if it's only a receptionist saying that their managing director never meets salespeople or that all purchasing is done centrally by their Athlone HQ. In some instances, you'll get a lot more information, although it may require you to probe a little. And you should probe a little. In fact, you should probe a lot. If you go back to the person who rejected you and ask them without emotional overtones to help you to learn from the experience, most companies are happy to provide that help. They'll indicate whether it was a money issue or a delivery-time issue or that they just went off the boil on the whole project. If you're honest with them, they'll be honest with you. 'I feel I did a bad presentation,' you can ask. 'How big a factor was that in your decision?'

If they say the presentation wasn't a factor, fine. If they say it might have contributed, ask them precisely what you did badly, thank them and, if you can, be funny about it. Don't make them feel tense and guilty – remember that this post-presentation conversation will stay in their memory and may influence some future decision. If they like you, they may be able to give you a consolation prize even if they're not, this time, going to give you a big contract. Or they may remember you warmly the next time a big contract comes around, not least because you asked for their honest opinion on your presentation. Remember that strategic selling is all about relationships. Even when there is no sale, the relationship should not go down the tubes with it. If you've failed to get the contract, a good post-presentation debriefing can a) give you useful information for the future and b) keep the relationship intact.

Some large companies have a slightly different approach to this important element of the sales process. They believe that the person who tried to make the sale is not necessarily the best person to do the post-factum research. For two reasons: the salesperson may be miserably self-conscious and defensive, even if they try hard not to be and the person at the other end of the phone may candy-coat the information requested because they don't want to hurt the salesperson any more than they've already been hurt. In this situation, an external consultant is brought in to make the visit (they nearly always go on site, which tends to get them more time and more information) and ask the questions. The theory is that the external consultant can have no agenda other than information-seeking, while the person working for the company that didn't make the purchase will be less bothered about handing on the bad news. The only downside is that it removes the possibility of an ongoing relationship between the salesperson and the executive in the other company.

Post-pitch debriefing should also happen when you win the contract or make the sale. Find out what you did right, because it is only by catching yourself doing things right that you can reinforce your selling skills.

All this comes with a caveat: some of what you hear from individuals and companies who have chosen not to go with your offering will be complete nonsense.

'You were right up there with the winning tender,' some may say. 'Only a hair's breadth separated you from them.'

Yeah, you want to say, but what the hell was the hair?

No matter how useless such feedback may be, you should nonetheless make notes of every call and every reaction. Once a month, do an analysis to see if any patterns emerge.

If you notice, for example, that most of the successful cold calls were made early on Wednesday morning, was that because you always go to the gym on the way to work on Wednesdays and therefore arrive at your desk buzzing and energised? Or was it just luck? (By the way, don't knock luck. Jean Cocteau said, 'We must believe in luck. For how else can we explain the success of those we don't like?')

If the majority of the unsuccessful calls happen late on Mondays, could that be because Monday is a particularly busy day for your potential customers – they are catching up after the weekend and wrecked by the end of the day? Or do *you* hate Mondays? Or you may note that towards the end of the month and especially towards the end of the quarter is a really hard time to make progress.

Whatever you learn, be ruthless with yourself. For example, go back to your take on each call and ask yourself what made you label one particular receptionist frosty and superior. What did you say that triggered their response? (Even if you said or did nothing untoward, clearly the approach you used didn't work so you have to try something else.) What will you do differently next time you call? Who can you talk to who might be able to help you with this?

This last bit is crucial. You should not battle with these issues or your own. Even in small companies, someone with more experience and expertise will almost always be available to you. Everyone in your company wants the business to thrive. They'll be happy to sit down with you. They'll be delighted when they see your systematic approach to self-assessment. They'll have enough of an insider's viewpoint to be rooting for you, while having enough objectivity to be able to give you realistic feedback and help you to come up with some new approaches.

Your procedure every time you hit a roadblock should be similar. Make out a list of questions for yourself:

- Why did this happen?
- How do I learn from it?
- What can I do differently?
- Who can help me?

The lessons you learn from analysing your cold calls and getting information about your presentation must be applied to all your encounters throughout the selling cycle. The secret of success in any walk of life is the ability to assess yourself realistically and make the changes you need to improve continually.

In addition to the feedback from your colleagues, you need to seek feedback from external sources. Erin Brockovich, the woman played by Julia Roberts in the eponymous movie, tells the story of how she did precisely this (quoted in I. R. Misner and D. Morgan, *Masters of Success*):

> I remember a long time ago when I was working for a company selling a shampoo line…One day a senior rep, who was evaluating me, watched me lose a sale. Afterwards, she took my pitch apart, almost word by word, and said

>to me, 'You know what, Erin, I'm impressed by your ability to take criticism so well.'
>
>'I don't see it as criticism,' I said, 'just another way to look at myself.' I'd ask the person who'd turned down the shampoo line to please help me help myself by telling me why. You'd be amazed how many people will take the time to explain the reasons for what they do and how often their actions have very little to do with you.

There's no need to be embarrassed about asking for feedback: people are delighted to be asked for their input. (Too often, they will give you their input without being asked.) Make it clear that you would welcome them helping you. You need to get their take on your performance to help you improve. If they give you general feedback, like, 'I wasn't sure you were clear about why we want to change suppliers,' ask them to give you a specific example of the point at which you betrayed that lack of understanding. You need to know specifically what behaviour of yours let you down. If you don't get specifics you won't be able to identify what to do differently.

All of this sounds negative whereas, in fact, most debriefings, particularly when you've won a contract, yield amazingly positive information. You may discover that you – or someone else on your team, if it was a team-selling exercise – demonstrated a skill you didn't know you had. Catching yourself doing something right is just as important for your ongoing self-improvement as catching yourself doing something wrong.

It's a little bit like a factor I constantly encounter when I'm training people in presentation skills. Participants get very worried about how often they say 'Eh' or 'Em,' and want me to give them tricks to avoid these fillers. I nod and ignore them, concentrating on capturing what they do well and spreading that more evenly throughout the presentation. Then I record a second version of their presentation. And you know what? The fillers fall away.

Whether you win or lose an individual sale, you should concentrate on what you did well, rather than obsessing over anything you may have done badly.

10

TAKING CARE OF CUSTOMERS

This chapter is not a standard piece on what's known in business as CRM (customer relations management). It's about trying to cut away some of the false accretions that have become attached to what should be a normal, civilised human relationship.

Customer relations management was practised by the banks during the boom years. Bank executives were trained (not by me) to contact customers regularly, seek out meetings with them and try to sell them products supplied by the banks over and above what they had already purchased. It was a selling exercise, not a care exercise. It sometimes worked and sometimes didn't work – in terms of flogging extra product. Where it clearly did not work was in establishing an relationship of real trust. If this had happened, when the banks hit Armageddon, lots of customers would have been coming out, talking about how wonderful their customer relations manager was. What actually happened, as we all know, was that credit dried up and the relationship went formal and punitive.

A different version of the same thing happens in some consultancy companies. At the pitch, the consultancy's

VIPs are rolled out to impress the potential client to death. The minute the sale is made, the VIPs disappear and a junior account executive is left in charge. Which is the business equivalent of getting married to the girl of your dreams and finding that her second cousin once removed has been substituted for the bride once the honeymoon finishes. Not good.

Taking care of customers undoubtedly needs IT support. Good intentions won't hack it: if you mean to have lunch with Client X now and again, to kick around ideas outside the agreed schedule of services, the chances that, worn down by the routine of surviving in a recession, you won't remember. So a computer program that flags when you haven't been in touch with your clients for a long time is a good thing.

For the most part, taking care of customers means extending the efforts you put into the five-stage programme to the ongoing relationship. These efforts include the following:

- You have to keep researching, so you're aware of changes in your clients' market as quickly as they are.
- You have to keep networking with the people who helped you before the sale, so they're clear about your continued commitment to what they helped you to win.
- You have to behave towards your customer as if they were your best friend – thinking about them and doing more than you're paid to do. Delivery of 100 per cent on contract is

> good. Exceeding delivery commitments by 110 per cent is good customer care.
> - You have to continue to listen.
> - You have to continue to capture what you hear. No, don't assume that because you found it interesting at the time you'll remember it. You won't, unless you have a central place (outside your brain) where ongoing information is stored.
> - You have to make your care of the customer real, rather than a form-filling exercise.

Form-filling is the most used and least effective method of customer care. Almost all hotels, for example, have little cards on a desk in each room inviting customers to rate the service they received. I've never seen evidence that these cards contribute to improving the experience of customers. The problem with these survey cards is threefold. The first problem is self-selection: the majority of people don't fill them in at all, so the few who do present a skewed picture of what customers really think. The second is that they are overly general, so that what they find out is an average reaction to the basic provisions. This is not worth a toss when it comes to further sales, either to that individual or to other people through that individual's intervention. If the customer who stayed in the hotel is happy that the bed wasn't made of nails, the bath wasn't full of algae and the pillows had a bit of puff in them, these factors will not persuade them to come back to the same hotel if they find one that's cheaper, cuter or nearer the venue for their meeting. Only something exceptional will outweigh these factors but hotel customer questionnaires don't emphasise the something exceptional.

The third inadequacy in the card-on-the-desk scenario is that it's not personal. It's supposed to move forward the relationship between the hotel and the customer. No relationship was ever moved forward by an impersonal card being left for filling in. A personal phone call from a manager, or the customer being asked by a staff member if they got anything more than they had expected when they checked in – these might do help to build a relationship but a card won't.

The central misapprehension about the card approach is that it starts from the seller's point of view, not from the purchaser's. Just as you tried to put yourself into the shoes of the customer before they signed up to buy your products or services, so you must put yourself into the shoes of the customer when you want to know how you're doing on their account. Or the slippers of the patient.

Florence Nightingale understood this about her own patients. Long after she came back from her period as the Lady with the Lamp during the Crimean War, where she cleaned up the hospitals to which injured soldiers were brought, she wrote an instruction book about nursing, called *Notes on Nursing*. Long before psychological studies of sick people proved her correct, she unerringly reached an understanding of what patients experience when they're facing surgery. She wrote:

> Apprehension, uncertainty, waiting and fear of surprise, do a patient more harm than any exertion. Always tell a patient and tell him

> beforehand, when you are going out and when
> you will be back, whether it is for a day, an hour
> or ten minutes.

Patients who go into hospital generally expect to have a clean bed, to undergo a procedure without having a swab left inside them, to be fed reasonably appetising food and to have their pain controlled. So asking them if the hospital delivered all those services to them is a complete waste of time as a method of measuring their satisfaction or dissatisfaction.

Where a patient has a choice of hospitals the next time around, none of those factors will bring them back to the first institution. What will bring them back is the nurse who took time to reassure them and make them laugh. Or the doctor who moved beyond her role and was particularly pleasant to their argumentative relatives.

Customer care is all about exceeding expectations, registering customer satisfaction with the specific actions that enable the expectations to be exceeded and making sure that actions like these are repeated.

Some form-filling is expected by customers in certain situations. People undertaking training programmes, for example, are commonly asked to fill in what are often referred to as 'happy sheets', allowing them to indicate what they found satisfactory or unsatisfactory in the training that the company supplied. In the Communications Clinic, we hand out these sheets and pay attention to the feedback that is on them. But, when a training programme is coming to a close and participants are completing their happy sheets, we tell them that when they need to refresh that special presentation, or they have a real, live *Morning Ireland* interview coming up, they can come in to us for an hour's refresher – free.

From where we stand this is an expensive offer. Many course participants never take us up on the offer, which makes it a bit less expensive. But they know we mean it and they know that there's no time-limit to it. In fact, there's often a substantial time-lag between the offer and when it is taken up. Once they leave our offices, participants in training courses are at once drawn back into the hectic day-to-day activities of their own companies and put the offer on the long finger. Or the need for training happened at exactly at the time it was needed and that need is cyclical, so they may not need refreshing for another six months or a year.

The longest gap any of our trainers recorded was eleven years between the original course and the delivery of the follow-up. In the interim, the trainer had moved from their original company but when the trainee tracked them down to their new employer, they were delighted to deliver. That's because our managing director, Anton Savage, is obsessed with the idea that we must always 'under-promise and over-deliver.' So we take a few minutes after every course to think about the individuals and consider how we could add value to their experience. Take, for example, the participant in the advance presentation skills course who was interested in great speeches of the past: let's send him transcripts of a few of them. Then there's the PowerPoint addict – we'll send her the reference for Peter Norvig (as cited by Professor Edward R. Tufte in The Cognitive Style of PowerPoint), who turned the Gettysburg address into a

PowerPoint presentation with results that were hilarious or nauseating depending on your point of view (see Chapter 8).

If you're in a service business, continuing to take care of your customers means thinking about what happens to them while the service is being provided and after the service has been provided. The relationship does not end when the service has been delivered. Correction. It *should* not end when the service has been delivered but, too often, it does. The customer pays up and is forgotten. That's fine if what the customer bought was a commodity that wasn't expensive and didn't involved any great thought or change in work practices on the part of their company. But if it was a service or a costly branded product sold to them in a way that registered their individuality, it is an insult to that customer to ditch them and forget them as soon as the cheque is lodged in your account. It's bad business, it's bad selling and, at a human level, it's the wrong way to behave. If a customer was worth being paid attention to before the sale, why on earth are they not worth being paid attention to after the sale?

Good salespeople find ways to continue to be useful to customers and to stay in touch with them. For example, you could be in a position to put individuals who might be useful to one another in touch, or to draw the attention of one to the possibility of a useful contact. If you can, do it. It is concrete evidence of your genuine interest, as opposed to the more mechanical method of taking people to lunch now and again or including them in a routine ezine mailing.

That's not to suggest that there isn't a case for emailing customers with updates on what you provide, since the simple act of reminding a customer that you continue to exist may land in their in-box coincident with them realising they have a need you could meet. But if you do such routine mailings, it's worth trying a) to make them as individually related as possible to the company or individual to whom you send them and b) to provide something within them which is of use, free of charge, to that customer.

Anything you can give a customer that's useful to them but for which they do not have to stump up is good. At any time. In a recession, it's twice as valuable.

If a customer contacts you with a complaint about your product or service, your reaction may be dismay but it should be delight. If your efforts to get to know them, truly understand their needs and become their partner, rather than a supplier, were genuine, any problem they have has to be your problem. When I talked to managers and sales managers in every sector for this book, I found a consistent emphasis among them that complaints should not only be occasions for learning but should be welcomed. Anne Heraty, CEO of recruitment firm CPL, says that while her company doesn't get a huge number of complaints, they have a clear philosophy that a complaint is a good thing, not a bad thing. Anne says:

> If nobody complains to us we just go along in blissful ignorance and they go and tell everyone else that they're not happy. So we're very open to complaints here and we take them on board and depending on the nature of the complaint, react to it immediately and try and solve it – do

whatever needs to be put in place to make sure that if we're in the wrong that it doesn't happen again or that's there's a solution for it. But I think it's hugely important to be open to complaints.

Jerry Kennelly of Stockbyte puts the same point rather more bluntly.

Honesty is the first thing. Where you say when it's great, celebrate it, when it's a fuck-up, it's a fuck-up. Just make it crystal clear. And point the finger. Rather than dodge. Weak managers dodge. Then everybody knows where they are. It's very important to be plain with people, to say that something went wrong. It's very important to create the environment where people can admit to making mistakes – making a mistake is fine, but continual mistakes is carelessness. I make loads of mistakes myself and I put my hand up and create an environment where I say, 'Look, I got it wrong.' That's gonna happen, but the post-match analysis is really important. That's vital, because the definition of insanity is doing the same thing twice and expecting different results.

Both in his general management role and in relation to selling, Jerry constantly finds himself referring back to a figure from his childhood in Tralee. This man worked for the Urban District Council and had the unenviable task of clearing blocked sanitation pipes. Jerry recalls:

> He used to have sticks tied to the bars of his bike and he had the nickname of Shitty Sticks. In our organisation, I'm Shitty Sticks, I've got to get rid of all the blockages in the pipes, because that's what a CEO has to do.

Clearing a customer's blocked pipes is a matter of overwhelming urgency if your service or product has in any way contributed to the blockage. The first thing to do is come out with your hands up. Don't tell the customer that this is the first complaint of its kind you've ever had. Don't suggest that it's their misuse of the technology that's caused the blockage. Acknowledge the problem, apologise right away and promise to sort it out – as soon as it's clear exactly what the nature and extent of the problem is. Find out as much as you can about the parameters of the difficulty before taking action, to ensure that the action taken will appropriate.

That's important. Not too long ago, the CEO of a large company went on television in the aftermath of the theft of laptops with customer bank details on them (unencrypted.) He apologised, very briefly, told us a number of times that all laptops were now encrypted (horses and stable doors sprang to mind) and finished with the slogan from the company's latest sales initiative. Customer care? Not as we know it.

On the other hand, there's the lovely example of an over-the-top response to a complaint from the American department store Nordstrom, which is a legend in customer care. A customer arrived in the store with a defective tyre. He was good and mad about the faulty tyre and told the manager he took a dim view of a company like Nordstrom selling him a dud. The manager apologised profusely and asked him if a full refund of the cost would solve the problem for him. Mollified, the customer nodded and the manager took the right amount of cash from a cash register and handed it over. Only when the customer had disappeared did a sales representative point out to the manager that Nordstrom don't sell tyres, so the customer couldn't have bought the stinker in any of their stores. The manager nodded and quietly pointed out that if the customer's belief in Nordstrom was dented by his perception that the company had sold him the dud tyre, good customer care meant removing his annoyance, rather than proving him wrong.

That's an astonishing level of response to a customer complaint but it's instructive. All the really good retailers we've worked with, from Superquinn to Marks and Spencer, train their sales staff to understand that a customer with a complaint is doing research, free of charge, for the store. They are bringing to the attention of the store something the store might otherwise have missed so they should, as a result, be warmly welcomed, listened to, learned from and satisfied. Research suggests that a customer whose complaint was dealt with superbly takes a better view of the individual or the company to which he complained than if no problem had arisen and will be more likely to recommend that company or individual to someone else.

Whenever possible, salespeople should have discretion to use controlled expenditure to solve the client's problem. But salespeople should be aware that a complaint is never merely a piece of equipment or an arrangement that's gone wrong. It is an emotional experience. The person who makes the complaint feels infuriated and diminished by the problem and the salesperson who is dealing with them must address these feelings as well as solving the actual problem. One great salesman I know makes it his habit, on the rare occasion on which he gets a complaint, to involve someone senior to himself. The more senior person may not be able to provide any better a solution to the problem than he can but the very fact of kicking the complaint upstairs establishes for the customer how seriously the issue is being taken.

Think of the stages in your apology and solving the problem as a series of gifts to your annoyed customer:

- The gift of attention: you are going to listen to the complaint and take it seriously.
- The gift of understanding: 'Oh God, that must have been so awkward for you...'
- The gift of speed: even if they've got through the immediate problem, a lasting solution should be speedily provided.
- The gift of certainty: you must make sure that they're confident it's not going to happen again.
- The gift of respect. Some salespeople give respect only before the sale. After that, to hell with the customer.

What customers with a complaint want is:

- To be listened to and taken seriously
- To have their problem and the reason they are upset understood
- Compensation or restitution
- A sense of urgency; to get their problem handled quickly
- Avoidance of further inconvenience
- To be treated with respect.
- To have the person who caused the problem aware that they caused it and to have appropriate disciplinary action taken if the problem is a serious one.
- To received an assurance that the problem will not happen again

Although the British comic writer P.G. Wodehouse maintained that it's a good rule in life never to apologise, because, as he put it, 'The right sort of people do not want apologies and the wrong sort take a mean advantage of them,' an apology, frankly and generously offered, always cements a relationship.

CONCLUSION

Happily, most of us in Ireland know the world has moved on from the hard sell. Finding and honing strategic selling skills is the challenge for most of us now. I've noticed that participants in sales training courses have most difficulty with the concept of initiating relationships and establishing trust. You'll notice I said 'concept'. These are the same people who, on first coming into our building say things like, 'These are lovely old buildings aren't they? Murder to heat in the winter though, I imagine.' Or, 'That's great coffee.' Or, 'Your directions were so easy to follow.' Obviously the *practicalities* of initiating relationships are second nature to them.

Most sales people automatically find something new, different or interesting to note about the office or set-up of the person they go to visit at stage three. Yet this is the area they find most unnerving when they think about it in advance – and the place where they would feel more secure if I could give them a handy formula.

There isn't a handy formula. If you don't trust your own communication skills in this (admittedly critical) first encounter, think it through. What do you know about this person? In a social situation, how much do you know about the people you meet for the first time? By and large, you don't find these first encounters nerve-wracking. You smile, shake the person's hand, ask a few questions, show an interest, and away you go.

Showing interest in the person is key. Focus on them, their company and their issues. Offer something. What you're offering must be of benefit to the new or potential client. It could be information, a useful contact or a free trial or sample. If it's a free trial or sample, it has to be of use to the person and their company. They must be able to see that you have thought about the company, its current situation and the challenges it's facing so that you know they value of what you're offering them. Once the offer is made, set it to one side and gently begin to find out more about their company and what they want.

Never forget, throughout all five stages of your sales process, that 'wants' count as much as 'needs', even though intellectually most company buyers focus on 'needs'. Needs are expressed in financial or commercial terms – 15 per cent increase in profits or 20 per cent improvement in market share. 'Wants' are inextricably linked with 'needs'. The buyer wants to look good to the board. Or they may want the satisfaction of eliminating most of the production-line delays so that the expense of delay is removed from their cost figures. There's always an emotional as well as a rational element to buying.

Focus on the relationship; hold back on pushing the product. Learn more about the industry and the company. Read, read, read. Question, listen and observe. In particular, find out what's different about the company and the people in it. Show your understanding of the differences and of the company's problems. Be flexible, be optimistic, seek feedback and get your own senior people to help you. The relationship will grow as trust grows. As David Maister emphasises in *The Truster Advisor*: 'trust must be earned and deserved.' So don't ever fudge an issue or tell a half-truth or dodge a question. You never earn – or deserve – trust without honesty.

Practise. The great pianist Artur Rubinstein once said 'If I omit practice for one day, I notice. If I omit practice for two days, the critics notice. If for three days, the public notice.' Each encounter is different: the day you assume it will be OK and wing it is the day you may damage a developing relationship. It is difficult and time-consuming to repair a damaged relationship. Much better to find yourself in the position where your champion is emailing you

'We've definitely got their interest…' This phrase was included in an email a colleague of mine received last week. He's been working with a senior manager from a very large pharmaceutical firm. The manager is very taken with our communications training and coaching and sees how much people from her company could benefit from it. Training plans are being drawn up for the year and she herself put in a proposal to her own seniors that they use the Communications Clinic. She emailed my colleague with the good news.

Note the 'We'. This manager sees herself and my colleague as partners in helping her company to make a worthwhile purchase.

That's relationship selling.

BIBLIOGRAPHY

Alessandra, Dr Tony and Rick Barrera. *Collaborative Selling: How to Gain the Competitive Advantage in Sales*. New Jersey: John Wiley and Sons, 1993.

Berry, Michael J.A. and Gordon S. Linoff. *Data Mining Techniques, for Marketing, Sales and Customer Relationship Management*. New Jersey: John Wiley and Sons, 1997.

Brooks, William T. *Sales Techniques*. New York: McGraw Hill, 2004.

Denny, Richard. *Selling to Win – Tested Techniques for Closing the Sale*. London: Kogan Page, 1997.

Hogan, Kevin. *The Science of Influence: How to Get Anyone to Say Yes in 8 Minutes or Less!* New Jersey: John Wiley and Sons, 2005.

Gladwell, Malcolm. *Outliers: The Story of Success*. London: Allen Lane, 2008.

Goleman, Daniel. *Emotional Intelligence: Why It Can Matter More than IQ*. London: Bloomsbury, 1996.

Goleman, Daniel. *Ecological Intelligence: Knowing the Hidden Impacts of What We Buy*. London: Penguin Books, 2009.

Gordon, Ian H. *Relationship Marketing: New Strategies, Techniques and Technologies to Win the Customers You Want and Keep Them Forever*. Ontario, Canada: John Wiley and Sons, 1998.

Heiman, Stephen E., Diane Sanchez and Tad Tuleja. *The New Strategic Selling*. New York: Warner Books, 1995.

Johnson, Spencer and Larry Wilson. *The One Minute Salesperson*. Glasgow: Fontana, 1985.

Koch, Richard. *The 80/20 Principle: The Secret of Achieving More with Less*. London: Nicholas Brealey Publishing, 1998.

Maister, David H., Charles H. Green, and Robert M. Galford. *The Trusted Advisor*. New York: The Free Press, 2008.

Misner, I.R. and D. Morgan. *Masters of Success*. Irvine, California: Entrepreneur Press, 2004.

Peoples, David A. *Selling to the Top*. New Jersey: John Wiley and Sons, 1993.

Prone, Terry. *Talk the Talk, How to Say What You Want to Say*. Dublin: Currach Press, 2007.

Rackham, Neil. *Spin Selling*. New York: McGraw Hill, 1988.

Richardson, Linda. *Stop Telling, Start Selling: How to Use Customer-focused Dialogue to Close Sales*. New York: McGraw Hill, 1998.

Rosen, Emanuel. *The Anatomy of Buzz: Creating Word-of-Mouth Marketing*. London: Harper Collins Business, 2000.

Sanchez, Diane, Stephen E Heiman and Tad Tuleja. *Selling Machine: How to Focus Everyone in Your Company on the Vital Business of Selling*. London: Kogan Page, 1998.

Taleb, Nassim Nicholas. *The Black Swan*. London: Penguin, 2008.

Tracy, Brian. *Advanced Selling Strategies*. New York: Simon and Schuster, 1995.

Tufte, Edward R. *The Cognitive Style of PowerPoint: Pitching*

Out Corrupts Within. Connecticut: Graphics Press, 2006.

Yankelovich, Daniel. *The Magic of Dialogue – Transforming Conflict into Cooperation*. London: Nicholas Brealey Publishing, 1999.